LIVE FAST
–DIE YOUNG

Remembering the Short Life of James Dean

John Gilmore

Thunder's Mouth Press • New York

Published by
Thunder's Mouth Press
632 Broadway, Seventh Floor
New York NY 10012

Library of Congress Cataloging-in-Publication Data
Gilmore, John, 1935-
    Live fast—die young: remembering the short life of James Dean /
John Gilmore. — 1st ed.
      p.   cm.
    ISBN 1-56025-146-8 (hardcover)
    1. Dean James, 1931-1955. 2. Motion picture actors and
actresses—United States—Biography. I. Title.
PM2287.D33G47   1997
791.43'028'092—dc21
[B]   97-13694
                                                        CIP

Manufactured in the United States of America
First Edition

LIVE FAST
–DIE YOUNG

*This one is for my wife, **Marie**,
with all my love and my appreciation.*

....

Author's Note

I wish to express my thanks to Debra Rodman, my friend and agent, and to Dick Smith in Texas for his encouragement, and once again to my longtime friend, Eartha Kitt. My heartfelt thanks to Dizzy Sheridan for sharing the past with me, and my gratitude to those principals I have quoted whose names appear throughout the text. To those individuals who asked that I respect their privacy, I have obliged their requests and those names have been changed.

What seems in order is a quick explanation on my sources for other information, quoted and otherwise, contained in this book. Sparing the reader a laborious list, I have presented here information based on my personal "living alongside the subject" experience. I had to make the decision that, in order to flesh out an emotional portrait, I'd have to lay the pictures clearly and without compromise.

Back in the 1970s, I was able to personally connect with some of Dean's relatives—not as a reporter or writer, but as one who'd been an intimate friend of Dean's. Other relatives, friends, and associates—some I knew professionally—were able to talk to me in an unguarded manner, comparing memories and sharing the gist of their involvements with Dean.

The Reverend James DeWeerd was one of the most helpful, the most frank and eager to share with me what he claimed was "in his heart," as he put it, along with Adelene Nall, Dean's former high-school drama coach. As the years have passed, other writers have not concerned themselves with what was in the Reverend's heart, but have done what I feel is a great disservice to James DeWeerd. I am thankful to this man, and others, and where my appreciation cannot be passed directly, I extend it in memoriam, as is now the case with James DeWeerd, and with Adelene Nall.

Much experience remembered in this text reflects the entries in notebooks I kept for years before becoming a writer. As a boy during the Second World War, I wrote on and off for close to half a century. Following Dean's death in 1955, I kept notations of things we'd talked about and shared. Thanks to my "Method" training as an actor, the sense-memory technique has proved invaluable for recapturing those long-ago moments that are now almost as real for me today as they were back then.

My primary focus with this work has been to offer an emotional portrait of James Dean as I knew him, consequently sidestepping some factual or informative data about the plays, television shows, and movies in which Dean participated. As well, I have shied from a more conventional or historical reporting on the social milieu in which Dean and I found ourselves, racing as though tomorrow was always a shadow just out of reach, beyond the settings in which our experiences took place. So this book represents a personal view of James Dean as he *really* was.

For a more objective accounting of themes and descriptions of Dean's professional work, I would invite the reader to consider Val Holley's book, *James Dean, the Biography*, for a fairly comprehensive listing of dates, reviews of plays, plots, and television shows. And perhaps for a more general, less personal view of the Hollywood and New York social climate of the time, as well as a sense of Indiana during Dean's younger years, I would recommend Donald Spoto's book *Rebel—The Life and Legend of James Dean*. These biographers have drawn up rather well-rounded accounts of the atmosphere in which Dean lived, and which he played against.

Perhaps it is the idea of *"against"* that thrust me upon this course. James Dean was a puppet of the time, fighting against the strings that held him; struggling to break free of restrictions and plunge himself through life as a frantic explorer in a never-ending jungle.

My efforts, then, have been to reconstruct the flesh-and-blood person, that speeding jester and most perverse person that paradoxically seemed to stand apart from the world in which he lived. It was upon this puzzle, and troubling theme, and a need to make some sense out of it, that I undertook the writing of this book.

—John Gilmore
Hollywood, 1997

Contents

James Dean's not our hero
because he was perfect, but because he perfectly
represented the damaged but beautiful soul of our time.

—Andy Warhol

*LIVE FAST
–DIE YOUNG*

Prologue

Dancing with Death

Dreams of the death car hang in my head. Weeks pass. Again and again I search the photo of the sleek Spyder as it looks before the crash—seeking some trace of its awesome destiny. Low to the ground like a coffin on wheels, the sections of blended magnesium curve in the sunlight as sculptured and smooth as polished bone. Faces around me are confused shells hollowed by the unexpected yet somehow anticipated tragedy.

It's now forty-two years later, shortly after five in the hazy afternoon. It was this time on September 30, 1955, that James Dean barreled hell-bent down an arrow-straight stretch of California highway, a gradual hill reaching westward into the sunset. The long road was broken by a T-intersection at the bottom where a black-and-white Ford came to a stop as if waiting to make a left turn heading north. Just those two cars in the middle of nowhere.

The joke still hangs in the air over the years since that fateful day; so many people stepping up to claim, "James Dean asked me to join him on that trip," which proved to be Dean's last ride. All supposedly declined the invitation. No one was waiting on the corner—including me. The others say some pressing commitment elsewhere or a sudden illness or abrupt inconvenience held them back.

They tell tall tales.

From the start of that trip north to run the new Porsche Spyder in a hot race at Salinas, the young German mechanic, Rolf Wutherich, a pal of Dean's since earlier that spring, agreed to ride shotgun so he could put Jimmy through some long-distance ropes as they rode. Two others—photographer Sanford Roth and an actor friend, Bill Hickman, were behind the Porsche, hauling the race car's trailer from the rear of a station wagon to truck the Spyder back to Hollywood following the event.

Years after that day, Rolf Wutherich would admit a different version to his often-repeated story of the car holding to the sixty-five-mile-per-hour speed limit. Saying he'd been paid off by "the studio" to keep the story clean, he said, "I'd tried to tell Jimmy since we left Hollywood that morning that he couldn't run such a new machine in that manner—like a monkey beating on something without considering what he might break. Jimmy would say one way to win was to go for broke. You had shoot it all, he said, you put it on the line and shoot it all...."

That September 30 afternoon, Rolf now says, "Jimmy drove like a crazy person. I said, 'Ease up.' He wouldn't hear me because he was out of view of anyone he supposed was watching to make sure he didn't get into trouble. 'Ease up!' I told him. 'I think you can kill *yourself* now but please do not kill *me* with you.'"

Rolf remembered Dean leaning slightly forward in the Spyder's small driver's seat—squinting against the setting sun down that gray pitch of highway. Both saw the black and white Ford. "It was hanging in the road down at the bottom of the hill in the other lane," Rolf recalls. "I know he saw us coming because he did not make the turn right away. It was like he was waiting...." And then the Ford inched almost imperceptibly into a left turn in front of the oncoming race car.

Jimmy said something, Rolf says. "It sounded like 'motherfucker'—because something was in his way, and I said, 'What did you say?' I didn't hear him!"

Dean's voice was instantly lost in the whine of the engine when his right foot jumped from the gas and hit down hard on the brake pedal.

It happened in an instant: The race car slammed the right front of the Ford in a shriek of tearing metal, ricocheting from the impact with Rolf being thrown from the car, his bones breaking as he hit the blacktop. The smash-up crushed the Spyder like a fistful of tinfoil and spun it off the road into a ditch with Dean slumped behind the wheel.

After hanging out with Dean on and off in Hollywood since earlier that same year, I'd left the coast in late July for a television show in New York, playing a kind of life-sized rag doll. Though I'd known about Jimmy buying the new race car, I'd only seen a snapshot of it a mutual friend had sent air mail. Jimmy had coughed up plenty for the car, having gone kind of nuts over driving sports cars in races in a sort of breakneck desperation to be first. He wanted to be crowned the winner. In an earlier race in the Speedster, the first Porsche he owned, he'd said, "I practically crashed across the finish first because I didn't give a damn how I got there and they all stood around with their mouths hanging open wondering how this *newcomer* beat their asses at their own game...."

We ran around Hollywood in his Speedster or the '50 Mercury I drove, or we screwed around with motorcycles—

taking off down the beach highway. But even then news articles and fan magazines were warning of Jimmy's recklessness. One magazine quoted a Warner Brothers spokesman as saying, "The crazy kid's going to kill himself...."

Jimmy laughed about it. He wondered what they'd put on his tombstone. "You remember the movie Bogart made—*Knock on Any Door*," he said, "and the line, 'Live fast, die young, have a good-looking corpse'? Shit, man, I'm going to be so good-looking they're going to have to *cement* me in the coffin!" I remember with that he cranked the gas with his right hand, popping the motorcycle clutch. The bike peeled ahead laying a strip of black rubber on the street.

I kicked the BSA ahead, tailing him; he was blowing smoke and the smell of gas stunk in my nose. Minutes later we came looping off Sunset Boulevard onto Highway 101 at sixty miles an hour. No cops. No speed limits were going to slow him down.

Jimmy hunched forward into the wind—I can still see that curved form, sort of lumped on the bike in black leather; the wire rims of the sunglasses pressing into his face. Racing ahead, he looked around, wagging me on. I opened my bike up. The ocean wind hurtled against me like someone sitting on my chest. I knew what he wanted. We'd done it once before, but now I sensed danger.

He said you could hit high speed and touch fingers across the gap of asphalt racing underneath us. There was a certain vibration from the hum of the plunging pistons. He said, "It's a barbershop quartet!" The feeling would rock through your bones and muscle and I remember him saying you could touch it like you'd touch a ghost.

The future looked bright and wide open as a prairie.

4
....

Though Jimmy only had been a recognizable movie star for less than six months (you'd have known his face if you'd seen *East of Eden*), a half year since the release of his first starring role, he was just twenty-four years old. The other two movies he'd starred in, *Rebel Without a Cause*, and the George Stevens film, *Giant*, with Elizabeth Taylor and Rock Hudson, were still unreleased when the new Porsche Spyder collided with that Ford in the middle of no man's land. The driver of the Ford, Donald Turnipseed, stepped from his car shaken but unhurt and stared blankly at the tangled wreckage of the Spyder.

Not far behind on the highway were Bill Hickman and Sanford Roth. The station wagon reached the wreck in moments and Hickman leaped out, climbed onto the tangled race car, and tried to lift Jimmy by the shoulders. He believed he could hear breath escaping Jimmy's mouth but could see no signs of life from the broken body.

Meteoric Star James Dean Dies in Crash. The news flashed around the world. Though crushed on the verge of great success— "nipped in the bud," the reports said, Dean's real stardom and world fame would begin with his death and the manufacturing of the myth.

No truer maverick have I ever known. He was a close friend before and during his brief, concentrated movie life. Shortly before his Hollywood recognition, we shared some lean and hungry days in New York, pounding the same pavement in search of the same game. On the surface it seemed the chase was just as important to me as it was to Jimmy, but with hindsight, it is clear he was more determined.

Obsessed with succeeding as an actor—of being crowned the winner—there was little Jimmy would not do to wedge himself into a television role or to get onstage. Acting is where he truly seemed to come to life. The characters he played on television, on stage and in the movies were hollow mannequins he filled with his talent. He was consummate at delivering a wholly rounded performance while the real person, outside of the character, often appeared as a "lost soul"—the impossible oddball, frantic or depressed, haunted by what he called a

5
....

"black mariah," some terrible dark wind he imagined blowing out of his past.

In the day-to-day world, the characters Dean portrayed were different individuals than the one that walked the New York streets with me or raced motorcycles along Pacific Coast Highway.

Almost dull at times or doped up on pot, appearing maybe infantile and stubborn, he'd milk the farmboy act to worm his way to advantages. He wasn't well-educated though he could don airs and spout verbiage, quoting T.S. Eliot, Antoine de Saint-Exupéry, or a spontaneous eruption of Alan Seeger's *I Have a Rendezvous with Death*, falling down as if dead at the end of the poem.

He got a bang out of dumb pranks like that, even dumber jokes about outhouses or jock straps, dreaming up bizarre things to shock and keep an edge on the perverseness that ran right down the middle of him like a core.

Back to poetry: He enjoyed it immensely but rarely read it or even held a book unless his picture was being taken. He liked to hear it read by others, and we'd sit in Greenwich Village coffeehouses listening to poets read their stuff. Incredibly, Jimmy would somehow remember chunks of these poems, reciting them at random—acting them out as some decrepit old man or any one of a number of funny-paper characters he'd mimic.

Bullfighting was another interest we shared, along with bongo and conga drums, preferably at our musician friend Cyril Jackson's place. We hung around with a few of the same friends for the year in New York; we had sex with the same girls, once with one of them in a kind of bizarre threesome. "Existential experimentation," he called it. We even explored sexual experiences with one another, though that publicized part of our friendship left a lot to be desired. Maybe it was to be fulfilled, to seek satisfaction or just to get smart.

The author screwing around and getting high in drummer Cyril Jackson's NY apartment. Photo by James Dean

For us the adventure, the chase was all. In order to make discoveries, he said you had to be willing to take the chances—the risks. Keep moving ahead, fast, or you wouldn't make the discoveries. I tried to keep up with him because he was pushing limits that had bound me in, but I wasn't pushing the same way. It would take a long time before I'd finally know how far he'd really gone.

Our intense friendship carried over from New York to Hollywood—though with a gap when I'd moved to San Francisco for a while—and until I eventually returned to the East Coast, hunting that elixir of excitement found only on the boards of the New York stage. So my relationship with James Dean was a sporadic, bumpy ride, often half-dimmed by our separate concerns and professional conflicts.

I'd been born and raised in Hollywood. I pretty well knew the ropes and the pitfalls. It offered an almost impossible path to travel without stumbling. Radio, television, and bit-part work in pictures were mine as a kid, for though my mother had been only a contract player at MGM, she'd had influential friends like Jean Harlow and Mervyn LeRoy, and she knew people like Dolores del Rio and even Howard Hughes.

Later in my career as a young actor, mentors such as Ida Lupino and John Hodiak urged my heading out for New York to avoid "the celluloid traps," as Ida Lupino called those holes in the road that's supposed to be paved with gold, the road they call "the boulevard of broken dreams."

As a would-be Hollywood renegade, and later "one of Jimmy's people," as a handful of us were called (or worse, "sycophants and malcontents," as the press put it), I managed to get myself a bad reputation: "an insurgent" with chips on both shoulders toward Hollywood.

This tickled Jimmy because he said he'd been through the same mill. "I've had my cock sucked by five of the big names in Hollywood," he told me one night. "I think it's pretty funny because I wanted more than anything to just get some little part, something to do, and they'd invite me for a fancy dinner overlooking the blue Pacific, and we'd have a few drinks, and how long could getting wined and dined and paying for it with your prick go on? That's what I wanted to know.... The answer was it could go on until there was nothing left, until they had what they wanted and there was nothing left....

"So *I* decided," Jimmy said with a Brando-like droop of his head, "they'd had all they were going to get—except this—"And he thrust his hand up with the middle finger standing straight.

Having nothing left was a frightening prospect, he said. "That's how you burn up—how *they'll* burn you up," he surmised. "But I'll burn it up myself and blow some gaskets in the process. You know—live fast and die young..."

Few saw Dean's dead body that fateful afternoon forty-one years ago in the small town of Paso Robles west of that highway intersection. Death hadn't been merciful to Jimmy, but came about almost instantaneously. At the same time, the abrupt end quickly ushered in another life—a phantom one, giving birth to the James Dean phenomenon almost as instantaneously as James Dean the person died.

"In all of our souls there are empty spaces that we want to fill," said Steve Allen on one of the many television specials about Jimmy, "and apparently in the American soul there is a vacuum at a point that Dean will fill...."

As one decade succeeds another, more specials and biographies on James Dean—whether paste-up or professionally objective, whether biased or self-serving, or simply hack jobs rehashing the profit-making, so-called legend—continue to offer the stereotype, to placate the reader with the mistaken belief that the question, "What was James Dean *really* like?" is being answered.

The true answer to that question has stayed in the shadows for the pieces of the puzzle that made up an individual as complicated as Dean remain behind a kind of screen separating personal experience from myth.

I do not want in this remembrance of Dean's short history to dwell on the myth or so-called legend, but to focus instead on the real life Dean lived. It was one, I believe, that passed too quickly and unevenly to allow for an orderly "objective" narrative to hope to fill that empty vacuum in the "American soul."

Stripped of the icon, unclouded by myth and supposition, this story for the *first time* gives a true portrait of the atomic-age maverick, James Dean, the chameleon-like, introverted oddball who was constantly charged by a streak of genius that sparked through him uncontrollably and without deliberation.

Jimmy had a terror of imperfection that was fanned by his

"black mariah." It made him unreachable by those he sought desperately to bring into his life. This fear would consume him, rendering him a zombie at times, full of loneliness and a glacierlike sense of desolation. I watched his desperation to succeed drive him into himself as he struggled to fuse everything he could know into one "glorious moment." He once said, "I'm seeing myself as Icarus going for the sun."

Three feature movies starring Dean comprise his major achievement. By the third and last picture, as his fame and success mushroomed, he was paradoxically, overcome with a devastating sense of failure. Having failed to measure up to his own standard of perfection, his personal chaos drew him to his end. In all ways, he highballed toward death with the same suddenness that attended his fame. Yet only in death would James Dean become perfect—a god-figure shining with indestructible perfection, the red windbreaker image of the perfect rebel without a cause.

"Like you have it all in your hand," he said to me one of the last times we spoke, "this thing you're after—and when you think it's right there you suddenly realize that you don't have it all...."

The only way to show James Dean as he really lived is to show him as he really was—grabbing for love and some measure of happiness while consumed by self-torture and anguish; a young man as withdrawn as Howard Hughes, shirking the spotlight but drunk on unquestionable fame. The only true view is through a glass darkly: his irresistible impulse to live life to the fullest—achieving perfection, coupled with a compulsive craving to "see the face of death...." Not God, but death.

He told me he sought to be as the bullfighter, dancing in the sun. "Noble and alone," casting a dark, long shadow, his eyes fixed to the bull's beady glare and steamy breath as the creature he fears "charges in for the kill...."

1.

Times Square

The first time I saw Dean he looked like a small scarecrow. It was the spring of 1953. I was sitting at the counter in a drugstore on Forty-seventh and Broadway, when he shambled in behind a guy I knew from the West Coast. Dean lurched into the place as though he'd tripped on the doorsill and was struggling for balance, a shock of hair standing out like straw. His hands were jammed into the pockets of baggy old gabardine trousers. A checked jacket hung on his slim frame like a sack with leather patches sewn around the cuffs. He had the air of a burlesque character, hunched down into himself, almost shrinking, and squinting through tortoise-framed glasses.

Ray Curry, the other guy, introduced Jimmy, who hung too far back for a handshake, so I only nodded and said, "How you doing?" He didn't say anything, just stood there staring suspiciously and bending slightly forward as though he had a stomach ache. Curry glanced at what I'd ordered, and asked the

By early '54, Jimmy was convinced he'd turn Hollywood upside down.

waitress to bring him the same—orange juice, coffee, an English muffin. He said he had to make a phone call and when she went to get the coffee, he pulled a big safety pin out of his pocket. Not too many people knew the trick—mostly struggling actors: you stuck the point of the pin into a mouthpiece, touch the clasp to the nickel or dime slot, and *presto*—a dial tone. Every pay phone wasn't fooled so easily, but the one in the drugstore and another in a booth in the Museum of Modern Art never failed to plug straight through, free of charge.

I was also wearing glasses, and after a few minutes Jimmy asked if I was nearsighted or farsighted. I told him I was farsighted.

"You're lucky," he said, sitting on a stool to my right. "You can read the fucking signs across the street."

Jimmy ordered the same as Curry, and while waiting for the juice, he twirled the stool between us, looking like he wanted to say something that I'd think was important. "Eyes can be a drag," he said, "if you can't see worth a shit and get up shit creek, man, without your spectacles." He went on to say he'd been in a Broadway play, but lost a pair of glasses during rehearsals and could hardly see the other actors if they "got out of reach."

"That's tough," I said. "You got to do without your glasses anyway—unless you wore them in the show."

Until he got used to the blocking, he said, he saw the others "only as shapes," and couldn't see how they were looking at him. So at first he related to the scene in his mind, "Not what the hams were doing on the stage," he said. I asked what the play was, and he said it was "a shit-kicker with Arthur Kennedy."

"But it was a *Broadway* play?" I said.

"Oh, sure," he said casually. "I was the best thing in it. At least that's what all the critics said." He shrugged. "But who

Jimmy said, "It's not real life I'm taking pictures of, but something that's already in my head." Photo of the author by James Dean/Jonathan Gilmore Collection

knows, am I right?" I asked him the name of the play and he told me—said, *"See The Jaguar..."*

I wasn't sure I'd heard of it, and he asked me how long I'd been in New York. "Not long," I said.

Suddenly his tone changed. "The play's the most wonderful thing I've ever done. You know what I mean?"

"Yeah," I said.

"I mean, I had more fun in it than I've had in working in a lot of other stuff." Leaning closer, he eyed the book I had open on the counter, Barnaby Conrad's *Matador*. He asked why I was reading a book about bullfighting.

"It's one of the few sports I like," I said. "That and boxing—"

He wanted to know if I'd read Hemingway's *Death in the Afternoon.* "Now *that's* a fucking book about *bull*fighting," he said.

I told him I happened to have a copy of the Hemingway book in my apartment. He asked where I lived.

"Around the corner on Forty-eighth off Eighth," I said.

"What've you got—a room?" he asked. "You got to come here to eat?"

"No, there's a kitchen," I said. "It's part of the one main room—the living room, I guess."

"You got another room there?" he asked.

"There's a bedroom," I said. "It's pretty small. There's a little balcony off the living-room windows that're over Forty-eighth, but it's just looking across the street at the fire station."

"Fire trucks coming in and out all the time," he said. "I know where that firehouse is. What about a *bath*room?" he asked. "You gotta take a crap in the hall?"

"No, I don't crap in the hall," I said. "There's a bathroom just off the bedroom. It's got a shower—over the tub, you know."

"It's better to take a shower," he said, "or you're liable to start piddling around with your dick if you get submerged in hot water..." He started laughing, and when I didn't join him in the joke, he said, "So, no shit, what's this apartment cost you?" I told him what I paid weekly and he said, "Sounds like you could stack up a couple more roommates in that much place."

"I haven't got any roommates," I said. "I had a guy living with me for a while, an English guy who teaches fencing. Right now I'm living alone."

Jimmy nodded, logging in the information. He never seemed to care where he lived, he said, and could sleep on almost any level surface. "As long as it's *flat!*" He asked if he could take a look at the Conrad book.

"It's a novel," I said. "Isn't anything like Hemingway's

15

Photo courtesy Photofest

16 .... Athur Kennedy said, "He's the most uniquely talented and peculiar person I've worked with."

book." He said he knew it was fiction. He knew the book. I slid it down the counter and he picked it up, holding it open in one hand. There were no illustrations but he hunched over the pages, looking at them as though staring at pictures. He touched the paper like someone reading Braille and his lips moved quickly, almost furtively. Every few moments he'd glance off as if remembering something or mouthing lines.

The drugstore provided thick pats of butter with its muffins and Jimmy helped himself to all the butter on his plate as well as Curry's, heaping it on the muffin which he ate with one hand, after which he'd sucked each finger clean. He said he'd gone down to Tijuana from L.A., to see the bullfights while a second-unit crew from Columbia Pictures, Jimmy said, were shooting a movie. An American matador named Sydney Franklin had been technical adviser in the picture, which he believed was *The Brave Bulls*, and gave Jimmy a cape during the filming, even though Jimmy hadn't been down there as part of the production. (He said Anthony Quinn was in the movie, and that he'd been "pals" with the actor since meeting him at a Hollywood party.)

"Why did he give it to you?" I asked. Jimmy said he'd met the bullfighter through some particular people, friends of Franklin's, then mentioned a matador by name, using the correct Spanish pronunciation, which is what earned him the cape. I said it was the same matador I'd seen gored less than a year before, not fatally, but bad enough to put him out of the ring.

"He was probably high as a kite," Jimmy said, and slid the book back to me. He asked if I'd seen the horn go into the guy, and I told him it all happened so fast I didn't actually see the horn sticking him. But he was on the ground in a second and the bull was going for him.

He nodded approvingly and without wanting to know if I'd

finished reading the book, he asked if he could borrow it. "You mean right now?" I asked.

"You think I'd mean later?" he said.

That's how our friendship began, with Jimmy borrowing a book I'd never see again. There'd be other books and authors, and we'd talk about them—Arthur Rimbaud's *Season in Hell*, García Lorca's plays, and Jean Cocteau. And I'd loan Jimmy another book called *The Psychology of Interpersonal Relations*. We'd talk about it, especially one section on memory and childhood amnesia which explained that we're conditioned to push back in our minds our childhood experiences. But when we'd discuss it a couple of weeks later, I could tell he hadn't read very much of the book. He finally confessed he was a slow reader.

"It takes me a while to get the gist of the whole thing," he said. "Like I have to study what I'm reading." Also because he thought in "circles," he said, grinning. "Going round and around.... Some people just think *square*, man."

I'd soon find out about his reading disability. Eager to talk about books, he'd absorb what was said, taking it in and quite consciously making it his own. It was an amazing trick, his sponging whatever you knew about a subject, kind of shaking it around with what he'd learned elsewhere, and then piecing it together into a rather original, persuasive presentation.

It took him a long time to read even one page. He thought in pictures, not in words I soon discovered. He would hear poetry read to him and what he'd picture would stay in his mind. He'd remember the pictures and could recite what he'd heard attached to those images.

Reading itself, though, was an excruciating chore and though he'd profess to be an avid reader, a "cosmolite," as he once put it, he rarely cracked a book. In acting, he had to "swallow the script," as he put it, "take it into the stomach and fart it out...." Without digesting the words, he'd mumble and stumble and say he was figuring out "motivations" and character, sort of rigging a kind of template over himself that wouldn't be right until it lay on his talents like a twin. All of which was a ruse, of course, to hide the reading problem. He had to absorb the full play before he could relate any of the parts to the whole. This would later create some serious problems for Jimmy, as his work became spotty, a collection of tricks and mannerisms. You'd be watching him pop through a series of bits like corn in a hot pan, and you wouldn't be taking in the character. At moments he'd appear as an isolated figure in a river of rush-hour traffic. "He'll have to control the idiosyncratic impulses," a television director said, "or go for a one-man show."

I talked to Curry for a few minutes after Jimmy walked out, hands in his pockets again, a cigarette dangling from his lips. He reminded me of the famous circus clown Emmett Kelly. Jimmy's eyes had the same look as the clown's: not funny or cheerful—more a sort of distant craziness. A controlled kind of craziness that kept you from knowing what he was thinking.

"He's a hot actor," Curry said. "You see him on television all the time." They'd met working as extras on a picture in Hollywood. As Curry talked I watched Jimmy through the window, waiting near the curb, his head craned back as he looked up at the building. "He's an oddball," Curry said. "We're going to smoke some reefers with this spade drummer.... You want to come along?"

It was too early, I said. I had a couple interviews. When Curry joined him on the sidewalk, Jimmy glanced back and gave a little nod, holding up two fingers. I didn't know what he meant by that.

19

The drugstore wasn't a popular theatrical hangout like Cromwell's Pharmacy a few blocks away, but was right in the heart of the "the Great White Way." An acting school and

63264

Tape recording a one-man bongo session in his Sunset Plaza apartment, early 1955.

dancing studio were nearby, and performers ran in and out swapping news, grabbing lunch or coffee. The Broadway show Jimmy played in, *See the Jaguar*, had closed after only six performances, but had gained him a rush of television work. One actress from the drugstore said he'd been "the best thing in a bad play," but was "an asshole in every other way it's possible to be...."

A few days passed until I saw him again at the counter drinking coffee and dunking a Baby Ruth candy bar in his cup. He said Curry'd told him I was related to the Gilmores of L.A.'s Gilmore Stadium where they'd held midget auto races. I said I wasn't, but my uncle had raced midgets and been a stunt man. That's what I'd told Curry, and Jimmy wanted to know if my uncle was still around. I didn't know.

Between his feet was a small cloth bag of dance togs from a class he'd taken. "It's body movement," he said, and told me he was working with Eartha Kitt, a sensational young actress/singer from *New Faces*. "She's my girlfriend," he said, smiling oddly. I told him I'd met Eartha in L.A. at the home of Alfredo de la Vega when she was doing *New Faces*. Jimmy said, "Shucks, man, I know that old queen. He wanted to suck my cock." Grinning, he said, "He must've wanted to suck yours."

I said, "Yeah, you're right. He's part of that whole crowd. It's the reason I'm here in New York instead of out there."

Jimmy named a couple of people from that same group and I nodded. "I know them," I said. He said I shouldn't feel bad—he knew them, too. He said not too many people were in a position to turn their backs on some of those who could get someone work. He asked if I was working at the time, and I said I wasn't.

When he learned I'd bought an old Norton motorcycle, he began talking about his high-school days and how he'd built a bike, then started putting together a hotrod. But then he'd

21

gone to L.A. "I should've come straight here instead of getting groped by everyone out there."

He asked if I knew James Sheldon. "He's about the best director in television," he said. "I'll introduce you to him. He's a fine man," Jimmy said.

Once we went to a Forty-second Street movie and sat through *A Place in the Sun*, and I slept through the last part the second time and when I woke, Jimmy was staring at the screen, missing nothing—his jaw muscles working as he chewed popcorn and Milk Duds, mixing them together. Other times he'd stuff his mouth with more than he could chew comfortably, and he'd gag and spit it out. A couple of times he flexed his lower jaw to loosen the upper bridge of his three false teeth.

His eyes were bloodshot as we left the theater and he didn't say much on the walk to Seventh Avenue. Then he began talking about Montgomery Clift's performance, and how Clift had put his work together even though we knew it was "all busted up" by the continuity of a movie. But it was "pure," just like a particular piece of sculpture that he considered "perfect," one with open ends, the same as Clift's acting in the George Stevens movie. "If you're going to do it," he said, "you have to work for the same perfection. It's there, you know, and once you get into it, all sorts of possibilities open up for you.... Shit, man, Stevens even made Elizabeth *Taylor* look good." After a few thoughtful moments, he said, "If I ever meet that woman I'd like to fuck her in the ass."

In a cafeteria near Broadway, we used the men's room before getting in the food line. Jimmy laughed about some holes in the wall between the urinal and toilet. He asked if I knew what the holes were for. I said I had a fair idea, and he said, "Do you know how to tell a sissy by his eyes?" I said I didn't know. He said, "Because he's got *high*balls!" I grinned but I didn't get the joke. I'd never heard it before or since, so I suspected it was something he'd made up on the spot, clowning around, a little dance step thrown in that didn't fit with what he was saying.

In Cromwell's he described the cartoon of a man in a small box who didn't like the world. He said it was the same as an emotional prison that few could escape. You had to "close up" and pull back in order to discover the truth about something, he said.

He seemed in his own world, yet gathered me into that same world as though into a conspiracy against a kind of outside he perceived better than I did. He could bring you in without your knowing it—if you weren't watching what was going on.

Eartha Kitt and I talked later about Jimmy's knack of pulling a person into a tightly episodic, one-on-one that had a way of running deep— disconcerting, if not downright disturbing. There were few pretensions. Jimmy seemed to demand in some hidden but direct way that you join him to form some single purpose.

Maybe that's what intrigued me most about him. Eartha said she couldn't remember going through any sort of "figuring out" of how he climbed into her life, or whether she liked him or not. "He was just suddenly there," she said. "I felt he'd always been there—one of the strangest friendships I've experienced...."

In the men's room, Jimmy squinted at the holes in the partition and touched them. He said they'd been drilled, not cut into the divider with a knife or some other tool. "Someone's come in here and *drilled* these holes!" he announced. Had somebody brought a brace and bit into the john? he wondered. Sat there drilling holes with his pants down around his ankles—as a cover in case someone came in? It seemed to matter to Jimmy how the thing had been done.

The all-night cafeteria was hot and stuffy, and Jimmy drank

coffee and smoked one cigarette after the other, lighting each new one from the butt of what he'd puffed down to his fingers. He hadn't told me where he was staying, even though I'd asked, but after a couple of these cafeteria sessions, he told me about "the flake and the chick," a situation he'd extricated himself from "not too long ago." He said some people could be baggage—"overfreight," he put it, that you couldn't "drag any further...." He told me he'd met "this particular guy" in L.A., at the UCLA drama school while he was studying to be an actor. They'd roomed together on the Coast, and then the guy followed him to New York, where the chick Jimmy had known hooked up with them. Joking, he said if one of them should die or "kill themselves," he'd be stuck with carrying the other farther than he wanted to.

In a short time I'd learn that wasn't the way the situation had been or how he'd really felt about it. Over the next few weeks of hanging around with Jimmy, I'd see the peculiar way he'd paint his scattered relationships, rarely as they really were. There was always the sense that he was hiding something—something urgent that he couldn't let anyone else know about.

One night in the cafeteria he asked if I'd seen any dead bodies in my travels, if I'd been close to death or seen people in caskets. I said only my grandmother in her coffin. He wanted to know what the coffin looked like, and I said I couldn't remember exactly, except the rails were shiny like the handlebars on my bicycle, and a different color than the casket. I asked him why he wanted to know and he dropped the subject.

At the time, I didn't know what his intentions were or why he'd ask things like that, except a couple of times he said, "You got to die, you got to die and you can't kick once you're dead." It was like the string Jean-Paul Sartre talked about, he said. "There's this string that's a person's life—*your* life—and these open scissor blades keep moving along the string—back and forth and where they'll snap shut nobody knows."

He leaned toward me and tapped his finger on the table. "I'm going to be the most important actor in town." His only worry was getting pulled into the army, a pretty serious blow to anyone's career. Being an actor, I knew a little about trying to get into Special Services and doing shows in the service, but Jimmy said one could beat the draft by claiming to have bisexual tendencies—"which includes having homo*sexual* tendencies," he said, "but a person's scared shitless of being branded a queer."

The Selective Service wasn't dumb, he said, pointing out that by telling them you were a bisexual, they'd see you were trying to hide the real facts from them, which "means you're as fruity as a flying eggbeater." he said, "It's like saying you've got only a little bit of leprosy." He hadn't been drafted yet because he was below 1-A due to his eyesight, he said, but he was above 4-F because he wasn't blind.

"They're not going to make you prove it by asking you to suck someone's dick," he said.

On our way out of the cafeteria he flirted with a woman at the cash register. He told her some joke I didn't hear and they were both laughing. Then a few days later in the drugstore on Forty-seventh, he approached the waitress with the same playfulness, when suddenly she called him a jerk for acting up. It was as though she'd knocked the air out of him. The brief incident bothered Jimmy a lot longer than it should have. He seemed to carry it around—a kind of nagging confusion he was working into some unnecessary grudge.

I didn't know whether he was trying to pick her up or not, or just do some kind of flirting number. He didn't seem to know how to come on properly to girls. Often he was rejected, though he'd seem to give up and turn away before he'd even gotten his foot in the door. Once he talked about it, saying he was worried about being accepted as "a regular guy," and not as the mind-boggling, emotionally confused "artist" he was. Chicks have to define the limits in relationships, he said. Men were easier. A cat'll lay a lot on the line for you. "A bitch won't.... She's always got an eye open for a better deal. Doesn't matter whether it's some other cat or a fucking break in her career. Get her ass ahead," he said. So he didn't spend much time trying to be "the okay guy" for the few girls who had their roles to live out, as he put it.

He had his share of detractors, other actors who'd say, "Oh, shit, here comes that little bastard.... Let's get out of here before he sees us." Of course, a couple years later these same people would allow as how they'd been his closest buddies, with tales to unspool like the ball on a runaway kite.

I'd met a girl named Miriam Conley who lived at the Barbazon Hotel for women. For a few weeks I'd been taking her on my motorcycle to modeling jobs, and a couple of times we had lunch in Central Park. We were walking my bike along the trail on the Fifth Avenue side one day, and saw Jimmy on a bench with another actor, Martin Landau. They were sitting at opposite ends on the bench, having some sort of argument. Jimmy was eating peanuts and had a camera strapped around his neck. He said he was going to take pictures of the monkey—I thought he was kidding Landau, who looked angry.

As we talked, Jimmy tossed peanuts at Miriam, throwing basketball shots to sink them down the front of her low-cut blouse. She laughed, caught some and threw them back. Jimmy thought that was great fun, and giggled while Landau looked resentful and kept urging Jimmy to leave. He stood up, tried to pull him by the arm but Jimmy said no, mouthing the word exaggeratedly, and kept repeating it, rolling his eyes and acting silly.

Disgusted, Landau said, "Okay, okay," and walked away.

Photo courtesy Jonathan Gilmore Collection

The author heading downtown, before 6th Avenue became Avenue of the Americas.

Though they were friends, Jimmy shook his head and looked at us, saying, "Who was *that* guy? Some flake, man!"

Miriam had never met Jimmy but she'd seen him on television and knew about the Broadway play and the radio interview where he talked about Aztec Indians. He wasn't at all shy about her flirting, and he began to joke around, jumping up on the benches and almost falling. Pulling a jacket over his face to look headless, he ran lopsidedly up the path, calling out "Ichabod Crane! Ichabod Crane! I want you!"

He collided with a woman and nearly knocked her over, scattering her packages on the ground. She was angry for a moment, but had to laugh as Jimmy, still headless, scuttled around picking them up for her. Then she opened her purse and gave him a dollar bill.

27

The monkey house at the zoo was a metal building with a tunnel through the center, bordered by cages. Jimmy was serious about taking pictures of the monkeys, and one in particular, a dark, noisy creature that kept reaching frantically through the bars. Miriam said she'd heard of monkeys biting, and Jimmy gave it a peanut, breaking the shell open with his own teeth. He wanted Miriam to be in the shot with the monkey, but teased her by grabbing her hand and pretending to stick it into the cage. She squealed and laughed. He took pictures of the ceilings and walls because he said the light was "dancing" up there. I sat outside on the bike watching them, Miriam giggling in a kind of false voice while Jimmy's attention focused on the monkey and whatever he was seeing through the camera.

I know Miriam saw Jimmy again and snuck him into her room at the Barbazon, strictly against regulations. I'd made it upstairs to the Barbazon lounge with her, and we'd neck when no one was up there but I hadn't been in her room. She once said she wanted to "kiss it and take it into her mouth," and unzipped my pants. She put her head on my lap and I placed her coat over her head. A woman walked by and I said the girl was sleeping——she'd been tired and fell asleep.

Once, heading down Eighth Avenue, he told me Miriam had gone down on him and "gives pretty good head." I said I knew that and he said, "I hope you're not hung up on the chick."

I wasn't, but I wanted to know if he'd fucked her, figuring he'd tell me if he had. He'd told me about a couple of girls I didn't know, one who hung around Actors Studio. But he said he hadn't fucked Miriam because she'd said she was saving herself for marriage.

"That's a crock," I said. She'd mentioned a guy from Wisconsin who'd gotten her pregnant and she'd started bleeding. She'd had it taken out of her by a scrape job at Bellevue Hospital.

"They all fucking lie, man," Jimmy said. "Females lie...."
He talked about the girl he'd been seeing awhile back, staying
with her half the time, Jimmy and the roommate he'd had in
L.A., until the girl "hightailed it for the woods...." He
should've played a trick on both of them, he said, by turning
himself into a regular hermaphrodite.

2.

Prelude to Destiny

He told me he could remember when he was a baby writing on a pink-colored wall with his shit.

"You can actually remember that?" I asked. He'd once participated in a sense-memory acting exercise at Actors Studio, and tried to feel the shit on his fingers, how it felt on the wall. It was a rough sort of wallpaper—sort of bubbled and hard—dried out, like air had gotten underneath the paper at some time and made it stand out from the plaster.

But he didn't remember where the place was—which apartment or house or whether it'd been in Fairmount or the town of Marion, a short ways north of Indianapolis where he'd been born.

Jimmy's mother, Mildred, worked in a Marion drugstore when she met his father, Winton Dean, employed as a dental technician at a veterans' hospital. Mildred's mother was dead, and her father, a farmer, had been hit hard by the Depression.

"There wasn't any money," Winton once said, looking back at his relationship with Jimmy's mother. "We'd go for walks around the town and maybe get coffee—maybe a scoop of ice cream if there was a few extra cents. I had to hold on or hitch a train heading to a bigger city where I knew times probably weren't going to be any better. Maybe it wasn't as bad in a little town as I was hearing it was just down in Indianapolis."

Mildred was "just the girl for Winton," and within a short time, she found herself pregnant. After a couple of months they decided to get married before Mildred's being with child looked too obvious "to be without a ring on her finger."

Six months after the wedding on February 8, 1931, Jimmy was born in one flat of a two-story wood-frame building on Fourth Street in Marion.

Though he remembered his diaper coming off, and writing on the wall with his fingers, Jimmy couldn't recall the number of places he lived the first few years or any of them that'd had that funny pink wall. The small family moved from small house to smaller apartment and once rented a flat above a store. When Winton was laid off from work, they traveled south to his hometown of Fairmount where they moved into a little cottage on his sister's farm.

A friend of the family would later say that Jimmy cried much of the time, had sinus problems and nasal congestion. He'd sometimes look like he was bleeding from his nostrils and have blood on his face from wiping at his nose and smudging the blood on the wall or the furnishings.

There were problems—"a lot of tensions between Winton and Mildred," that weren't talked about....Winton complained that the baby kept crying and he believed the solution lay in spankings. But the baby cried just the same.

Though Jimmy's mother later became the boy's nurturing symbol, the young woman was "a very nervous person, very easily set off." A relative claims Mildred would "jerk the little boy by the arms at times....Grabbing him up by an arm and shaking him so hard his feet'd be kicking off the ground.... The baby had to go to see the doctor a few times because of the bad bruises."

The boy's aunt thought the child was bleeding under the skin, that he had some uncommon ailment. The family doctor assured them that he'd outgrow whatever problems seemed to be plaguing him. A recommended "blood tonic" was added to his food in small doses and mixed in with his bottle. Jimmy was still frequently taking his meals from the baby bottle because, as Mildred told an in-law, "He often throws up the solid food or he has diarrhea...." He'd lost weight and grown pale. "When I give him a thicker mixture in his bottle," Mildred said, "he takes that down and naps for longer periods of time...."

Jimmy was almost three when Winton moved them to Fairmount. During the year that followed, Winton tried unsuccessfully to find work. "Some people thought of killing themselves," he said. He was finally called back to the hospital where he accepted an offer to relocate to the Sawtell Veterans Hospital in Santa Monica, California.

Jimmy turned five years old when the family settled in a small house on Twenty-sixth Street in Santa Monica. Since childhood, Mildred had studied the piano, and she'd also practiced the flute. An avid reader, she often walked Jimmy to a neighborhood library where she'd browse the poetry books. The poems she had composed in Marion had somehow not survived the move west. Mystery has always clouded Jimmy's mother; she seems to have left little of herself in the world, most of it invested into Jimmy's memories. But from what is known, she emerges as a sensitive person believing herself to be out of place—as though born in some other time and place and abandoned on a farm in Indianna.

She was easily influenced and had inclinations toward the

ethereal. The poems she wrote apparently explored the loneliness she felt as a girl on the farm. She'd mention weathered walls of barns, and once wrote a poem about a pig too fat to get through the fence gate which got its head stuck and strangled.

But like Blanche DuBois in Tennessee Williams' *A Streetcar Named Desire*, Mildred seemed to shrink from harshness and carried a faith that she might somehow realize her dreams through her son. The boy was so willing and so interested and the special moments they shared seemed to enable her to live more comfortably with the sense of futility and depression she mentioned in her letters to Marion.

In Santa Monica she soon began to compose poems again, which she'd read to Jimmy who was happiest at home with his mother. When alone with him (with his father away at work, Mildred's nervousness would seem to lift away), she tired easily, though. She'd often stop walking, saying she was short of breath. She'd lay on the couch, her eyes closed, and Jimmy would sit on the floor with his back against the side of the couch, drawing pictures or holding her hand while she slept. Often she'd invite him to sing some of the little songs she had taught him. Slowly, he was learning to play the violin, and the two of them went on small picnics and imaginary strolls into gardens of make-believe.

At night she read him stories, hoping to improve his ability with words. He resisted the printed text, but drank in the sound when his mother would read to him until he fell asleep. Years later, Jimmy said he could recall images from those stories, and said how they'd return occasionally just before he dropped off to sleep.

In 1937, his mother enrolled him in kindergarten but it was not easy for Jimmy to make friends. He was an able pupil, polite enough, and displayed "a peculiar determination," as one teacher recalls, "to see that things were going his way and that he had some control over the others...." At times shy and "even skittish," he avoided joining into groups, and as another teacher says, "The impression he gave was that he thought he was being punished by having to attend school. When told there were many things to learn in school, he said he could learn more at home than he could be taught in school.

If criticized, Jimmy was easily brought to tears. He told his mother that some children who had done something wrong were taken to the office, where they were spanked with a big paddle. It was called "getting swats," one teacher had said to him, and for weeks Jimmy seemed anxious that such a fate was going to happen to him.

More than once he ran away from school, before the day was finished. His mother didn't make him go back and she didn't tell Winton. She knew he would make Jimmy "turn right around and get back to school," but Mildred was more concerned with Jimmy's need of the closeness only she seemed capable of offering him.

Once he was invited to a nearby birthday party where the neighborhood kids had gathered for a Saturday afternoon. Placed about on the floor of the house were fancy porcelain figurines and silver picture-frames with old people's photographs and glass dogs and teacups. The other children were about to blindfold him, the point of the game being to successfully thread one's way through the maze without seeing what was underfoot.

Jimmy didn't understand the game and panicked. His fear caused the others to make fun of him and instead of facing up to them or taking his chances with the blindfold, he ran away from the party. He later told me he could still remember how hard his heart was beating as he ran, and how his footsteps sounded like wings beating about his head.

At home he tried to tell his mother of his fears and she'd try to distract him by having him practice the violin. More stories would be read, with Mildred energetically acting out the characters until Jimmy'd giggle. When they'd laugh together his tears would be gone.

Aside from going to school, most of his time was spent being protected by his mother; looking forward to music lessons, and to having poems read to him—a behavior that caused his father to believe that his son had unmanly tendencies, was not a normal boy, and Winton would soon separate himself from his son.

Jimmy once said of him: "I never understood him. I never understood what he was after or what sort of person he was because he never tried to get on my side of the fence, or try to see things the way I saw them. I was always with my mother and we were very close. She used to turn things in the water for me"—it was when he was taking a bath—"she used to put this little boat I had in the water, and then she would make the water turn like a whirlpool by turning her finger around and around the boat....It used to make me dizzy! I'd laugh and laugh and I wanted to do it myself, but what happened was that I would start turning the water around and the boat would flop over upside down and it'd sink. I never understood it—how she could keep it from sinking."

Winton frequently complained that Jimmy seemed "girlish" at times. No "red-blooded boy" should be satisfied to spend more time with his mother than with playmates his own age. Later in life, depending on who was around, Jimmy would boast about the closeness he shared with his father. But he was never able to keep the truth from himself. Because Winton was unable to show enthusiasm for the violin lessons, or the tap dancing, or the poetry his mother read or the stories she'd tell him, Jimmy withdrew from his father, who, though aware of the distance between them, made little or no effort to close it. And with the increasing coolness between Winton and Mildred, for Jimmy the differences were to prove irreconcilable.

Though weakened by illness, Mildred had entertained ideas of leaving her husband, of packing the few belongings and with Jimmy in tow, "hightailing to some exotic land" where they'd find happiness. She'd never really been happy and she wanted something drastic to happen to her. These were frantic thoughts creating unbearable confusion, she confided to a neighbor. She seemed confident that a better life was possible if only she could manage to arrive at the way to attain it. Once she said, "Jimmy is all I have in the world, and God knows I'm all he has."

Jimmy, whose middle name was Byron, later told us all: "My mother named me after Lord Byron...." and he liked to tell about how he was a child prodigy. Despite his father's reservations, he was an outwardly normal boy in most ways, and yet, like Kierkegaard, he was coached into imaginary settings by an adult. Jimmy's mother used to make up nonexistent scenery in the living room. "See the pretty waterfall?" she'd say, and he would squint and make-believe it was there. "Yes, yes. I see it!" He'd later say that he shared with the founder of existentialism an approach to life that was significant to the American art, music, and literary world, namely that if one chooses to believe in something hard enough, it will make itself come true. At one point, Mildred and Jimmy even made up private words to speak to one another in a secret language.

The lack of acceptance by his father troubled Jimmy deeply the rest of his life—as did his relationship with his aunt and his uncle, who never really *answered* him, but only tried to "help" him. "It was [like] someone dehydrating in the desert," he once said, "and what you're getting is a bowl of cornflakes." His grandparents, too, were not aware of who he really was. He'd spend the remainder of his life searching out substitutes for the acceptance—apart from his mother's—that he never received as a child.

When he was eight, Mildred became sick. She was not yet twenty-nine but had severe chest pains. At first, because of the the loss of weight and the constant fatigue, she suspected a heart condition, believing she was having a series of small heart attacks or some form of stroke. But X-rays uncovered the truth. It was ovarian cancer, and further examinations revealed the disease was too far advanced for hope of recovery.

"Please do not tell my son that I am this seriously ill," she begged. "He cannot know that I am dying!"

She was hospitalized and a number of treatments were undertaken but her condition grew steadily worse.

Winton agreed not to tell Jimmy that his mother would not be getting well. Secretly, he had long since tired of his wife and was sorry that he married her. He once said that he wouldn't have wed "such a frail woman" if she hadn't become pregnant. That same frailty or weakness, as Winton put it, was mirrored in their child. An associate of Winton's at the veterans' hospital would later mention that Winton once said some possibility existed that the boy was not Winton's own child.

Coupled with these notions was another, that he'd be stuck with raising a child he believed he could not tolerate, not to mention that the "kid" was probably a "little bastard."

Hastily, Winton wrote to his mother in Fairmount, telling her that his wife was ill and in the hospital. Jimmy knew nothing about her condition, he said, claiming that it would be impossible to tell the boy that his mother was dying. He suspected in some way Jimmy might hold *him* responsible for her never coming home. Jimmy and his mother had been "too close—abnormally close," Winton said, and while he'd tried to get close to the boy, too many problems between Winton and Mildred had stood in the way.

He told his mother in Fairmount that the work situation with the VA was unsteady. This was untrue. Things were so bad he said, that "I'm hanging onto just staying alive by my fingernails." However, the most difficult prospect he faced was that of "surviving" with Jimmy, but without Mildred to take care of him.

Winton's mother came out from Indiana to look after her grandson while Winton held his job and waited for his wife to die. "I couldn't tell the boy," he said. "He just looks at me, stares me in the face. Whatever I'd say, it's like he didn't understand what I'm saying. Even if I hit him, he closes his mouth and narrows his eyes and he won't say a word...." Winton once said, "You have to be strong to live" and said he couldn't have a weakling for a son. Jimmy would never forget those words or how they were delivered—as hammering down the lid of a coffin.

When Mildred died, Winton had her body shipped by train to Indiana. She was buried in Marion with all the funeral expenses paid by her family. Winton didn't want to spend the money. He decided to ship the boy back to Indiana along with the body of his dead wife. Jimmy could live with Winton's sister, Ortense, and her husband Marcus Winslow in Fairmount.

Mildred's coffin was loaded aboard the Challenger bound for Indiana. Winton's mother Emma ushered the nine-year-old Jimmy onto the same train leaving California. Winton would not make the journey, nor would he travel back for his wife's funeral six days later in Marion.

With no idea of his father's plans or that his life was to alter so drastically, Jimmy sat beside his grandmother, worried that the coffin might get lost on the way to Indiana. Whenever the train stopped, he insisted on going to the baggage car to make certain that it was still on board.

Later he was to recall feeling then that if he'd also been dead there might have been a completeness to the picture. "Your mother is now with God," his grandmother told him. That meant she was no longer with Jimmy. Later he recalled experiencing something then that "seemed worse than dying itself." He felt stripped of everything—exiled without knowing why—except that he was with his mother, even though she was dead and in the box in the baggage car—maybe something worse than his mother having died and his being left alone. He'd felt compelled to know where they were on the train, to know every detail of its cars—each mile of track, each telephone line whipping past the windows. He didn't want anything else to get away from him.

He'd suddenly lost both his parents without knowing how or why, or the real reasons he was being sent back to Indiana.

3.

Indiana Twilight

There was hardly anyone at the funeral the day Jimmy's
mother was buried. Only a few relatives stood at the
grave in Grant Memorial Park Cemetery in Marion
watching the coffin being lowered into the ground.

It was difficult for the young boy to grasp that his mother
wouldn't be coming back up out of the earth—that she was
going down into it for all time to come.

After the service, his aunt Ortense and her husband Marcus
took the boy to Fairmount to live with them in a large farm-
house on their good-sized spread. There were hogs, cows, and
acres of oats and grain. His grandparents lived on the out-
skirts of Fairmount on their own smaller farm.

Anemic almost to the point of illness when he first arrived
on the farm, Jimmy's condition was attributted by the
Winslows to the upheavals he'd been through—his mother's
death and the separation from his father. "Nobody could blame
the boy," his aunt said. "He'd been cut off from everything."

Jimmy would say later he never wanted to live on a farm. But what choice did he have? One thought stuck in his mind—getting back home to California.

From that point on, Jimmy kept his real feelings a secret. Home had been where his mother died. Everything he thought he understood was in California and all he had to do was find his way there. The picture was clear: the stucco house, his mother on the couch; she'd look up as he walked toward her and he could imagine a soft sort of light shining out of her eyes.

He'd wonder how much dirt would be piled up on her face in the grave. Her eyes would be covered with earth. She'd be blind and she'd never see Jimmy again.

"A few times I dreamed of going to Marion where my mother's grave is, and it'd be twilight. I'd get to the cemetery and she'd be standing on the ground like she'd come up out of it and was waiting for me...." As he'd walk toward her that "glow or light like something that's phosphorous would be shining from her eyes...." Slowly she would lift her arms upward to embrace him.

"You couldn't tell Jimmy not to imagine what he was thinking up," his aunt said. "It went on like that for a long time. The little fellow seemed to be making it hard on himself, like he was singled out and held accountable for what had happened.... He had a lot of changing to go through, but he saw soon enough that he'd have a good home with us.... A better home than what he'd had in California."

It was an unfortunate situation; there hadn't been anything he'd been close to except his mother. And now the dreams. In another, he said, his mother was trying to sit up in the coffin but couldn't because the lid was closed. Jimmy imagined he could hear her hammering against the lid with her hands.

Things began to change the following year, though. As if guilt was something Jimmy struggled against in himself, he also showed a marked determination to outdo others. Once he overcame a fear of drowning, he learned to swim in the creek, and soon was playing baseball, running the fastest and farthest of the boys his age.

Meanwhile he'd learned to work the farm like an old hand, tending stock and living like "a regular Midwestern Quaker," his aunt recalled, "Hoosier through and through." And yet as he grew past the age of twelve, he seemed to be as much at home off by himself with a tree or a post or a goat.

He told his aunt he could talk to the tree and she said, "Well, don't tell nobody else you're talking to the trees or they're liable to think you're crazy."

"Only one tree," Jimmy said. He said he could talk to the trunk of the tree and his voice would go into the wood and down to the roots. His voice would then spread under the ground.

"I remember him sitting at the kitchen table eating a sandwich, and I said, 'Well, Jimmy, that is real interesting. Does the tree roots answer you back, son?'"

He wasn't talking to the tree or the roots, he said, laughing. "I said, 'Well, who're you talking to?'" his aunt recalled. "He just looked at me with a clean face and said, 'My mother.'"

Believing he had to look out for himself, Jimmy made every effort to learn what he could, to handle tools and fix machines. His uncle says, "He'd try to do something, fixing something, or later in high school tinkering with a motor scooter or that car they were taking apart and running it up and down. Half the time it wasn't running, but Jim only seemed to get more determined. Something of the perfectionist in him like with his granddad Charlie, something inherited in having to make something a certain way and being perfect. But each time Jim did it, no matter what it was, it'd come out different. Frustrating him something terrible."

Joan, the Winslows' only child, was five years older than

Jimmy and more like an older sister than someone he could play with. His life differed little from day to day, and his aunt and uncle chose to see it as "just like anyone else [is] here—a simple life like most of the people in these parts. Simple people in that we are close to the land and farms. That is what we are dedicated to."

Years later, at the Hollywood Ranch Market, Jimmy was eating chocolate doughnuts and talking about his aunt Ortense when he suddenly said, "But you have to understand I was like what you'd call a schizoid personality…." He said he was "sort of two people in the same skin…." He could see it in himself—sense it, one self telescoping back from the other. One lived on the "outside" and the other kept himself hidden. On the farm, he hadn't been able to sleep without a light burning or someone else sleeping in the same room. In the dark, he said, the person hidden inside would seem to drift up to the surface of his skin, but the closer it got to getting out of him the more desperate it'd make him feel. It wasn't anything that'd creep up on him out of the dark that he feared, but the fact that there was no light and he couldn't see. He imagined the dark as a kind of blanket no light could shine through, and it would cover his face. Keeping him from seeing or breathing, he'd panic.

Pampered by the Winslows because of the "problems he'd had back when he was child," his aunt and uncle avoided the subject of his mother's death—"as though she'd never lived," and the unexplained separation from his father.

Fairmount would prove a kind of a hinge between the past he feared and the uncertainties of his future. He realized he'd always wanted out but never "ran away because I couldn't hurt those people that saved me."

As though afraid to stay in one place too long, Jimmy began shifting from club to group and through different sports teams—short-lived connections; knots he tied that quickly unraveled. Those he apparently sidled close to were often the oddballs, in some way the socially castigated, usually older than Jimmy and considered "peculiar" or "different" by townsfolk. Such a one was the local evangelist preacher, Reverend James DeWeerd.

An interesting if perhaps eccentric bachelor in his mid-thirties, DeWeerd was always thought of as a "scout master" by the boys on the high school basketball team. The preacher often took them swimming or to an auto race, frequently hauling them to games in his fancy car. Some he taught to drive.

Sometimes he'd invite several boys to his house for dinner and show home movies of trips to other states, including a film from Mexico that included some bullfighting scenes. The evenings sometimes closed with DeWeerd reading from his own poetry and also the work of the famous war poet Alan Seeger, especially his masterpiece, *I Have a Rendezvous with Death*.

"A couple of times Jim would be repeating the words of poems along with my reading aloud," DeWeerd said, and he asked if Jimmy knew them. "He said he remembered the lines because of the way I read—not that he'd gained it from reading the texts on his own...."

"He liked certain sections of the Bible," the preacher said. "I was reading once and he started repeating it the same as he'd done with the poems, only saying the words aloud along with me. We did a little test—who could sound the most dramatic? I'm sure he won our match; That bright, enthusiasm he'd show let you know he was getting a big kick out of everything."

Exaggerated accounts of the preacher's bullfight movies have spanned decades, but in fact there was only one that facinated Jimmy—the half-hour short with the bullfighting footage representing only one segment of DeWeerd's Mexican holiday reel.

The Reverend James DeWeerd, Jimmy said, "was a shining light in my fucking life, like one of those beacons on a dark island."

Jimmy was "engrossed [in] the scene of the matador and the bull," DeWeerd said, "especially the bullfighter caught by the bull's horn and dragged a short distance. Another shot showed a different matador killing the bull with the sword, which is done at a difficult and dangerous angle where he has to go up and over the horns of the bull in order to place the sword. The poor animal drops to its knees then rolls over dead...."

DeWeerd was not an avid bullfighting enthusiast, but he said, "Jim went for it in a big way.... Something more than a simple morbid curiosity, though it was that, too. He wanted to see it over and over again, and perseverated on those rather brutal or gory scenes."

To DeWeerd Jimmy was somehow different from other boys. His energy was running away with him and had to be harnessed in a constructive way. It was brewing things beneath the surface, "eating at him," as DeWeerd put it. He wanted to keep Jimmy out of trouble, the preacher said.

Then Jimmy approached DeWeerd to talk "about some personal things...." He understood he could say things to the preacher in confidence and asked if it would be like confessing to a priest." DeWeerd said no.

"Instead of a confessional box," DeWeerd said, "we had lunch together," and when Jimmy felt comfortable enough he said he believed the ghost of his dead mother came to him. The dark scared him, he said, and he was afraid he'd suffocate as if being buried alive. When his mother "came" to him the fear would be taken away.

DeWeerd said, "He seemed to be carrying some self-imposed responsibility for his mother's early death." Jimmy suspected that his father felt Jimmy had played a hand in taking Mildred's life as if she had been killed—murdered by some circumstance Jimmy thought he was "bound up in." His father hated him for it, Jimmy told DeWeerd, so that he—the son—was as dead in his father's eyes as was the boy's mother. He believed it was the reason he had been sent away along with his dead mother.

Jimmy continued to talk to DeWeerd, but the father figure he'd found in the preacher was soon replaced by a kind of mother figure in his high school drama teacher Adelene Nall.

Coached by Nall in public speaking, Jimmy by now sixteen years old, placed in a statewide speaking meet sponsored by the National Forensic League. The local newspaper headlined his victory in a front-page story. "It seemed the most important event in his life," DeWeerd said. "A magic door had opened for him."

Jimmy handed copies of the newspaper to everyone he met, and soon moved onto acting in school plays. His whole being was put into motion by the involvement onstage. There, his energies worked for him and it felt *good* to command attention and experience power and a sense of manipulation.

"The whole place could be in my hand," Jimmy said. "In my personal control, everyone out there, the people and the others on the stage with me—it's like I was the sun in a universe. I could be giving life to all of it."

Soon Jimmy was nicknamed "Fairmount's fair-haired boy," with each debate or acting role played up enthusiastically by the newspaper.

He became exceptional, says Adelene Nall, "and he said he was giving serious thought to being an actor...." He told DeWeerd, "You know what I'd *really* like to do? Go back to California and get into a theater arts program," like the one at University of California in Los Angeles. "He said he could even try to land an acting role on radio or television to keep himself solvent while going to UCLA."

Through DeWeerd's urgings, Jimmy resumed contact with his father. He wrote letters to Winton, enclosing his newspaper clippings and explaining in detail the plans he was making for a future in acting. "I felt if he looked honestly into the man that was his father," DeWeerd says, "Jim wouldn't find the hatred he feared would be there, but rather a man probably as awkward as his son at expressing what he *truthfully* felt...."

Jimmy graduated high school in the spring of 1949, and in an overnight decision, he began preparing for a move to Los

Angeles. It seemed reasonable to live at his father's house, using that as his "home base" and curbing expenses. He told the preacher and Adelene Nall, "My father says it's a good idea. He's receptive to my staying with him while I go to school."

Prompted by DeWeerd, he wove a picture of a happy reunion into his plans. He fancied exchanges of forgiveness, with father and son both understanding the loss experienced in the past and hopefully, merging their lives for a bright tomorrow—a dream to be repetitively playacted whenever Jimmy talked or wrote to his father.

Meanwhile, Jimmy'd found another Fairmount oddball in Bette McPhearson, older than he and somewhat of an outcast. She drew his attention the same as the preacher had, by reaching beneath the "guards" Jimmy used as hidden shields of battle. Bette invited Jimmy to her home often to drink beer and be read to on her couch with his head in her lap. Her hand would be stroking his head and face as she read. "I lost my virginity in Fairmount" Jimmy later told me "before I came out west to become a whore...."

Fairmount threw a party in Jimmy's honor following graduation, with schoolmates, relatives and townspeople wishing him well. Then wasting no time in putting his plans into action, he left town on the next Greyhound heading west for Los Angeles.

4.

Riding the Merry-Go-Round

66 **I** knew within five minutes of being back in Santa Monica at my father's house," Jimmy told me years later, "that it was a miserable, rotten mistake. Like being told somebody's going to hang you thirty days from today...."

He believed the hatred he felt for Winton was returned. No amnesia to numb the bitter memories. The ill feelings Jimmy would later spew at others often emanated from that same "root that got stuck" in his stomach—from the one who'd made his mother pregnant.

Winton had remarried four years after Mildred's death, lived in another stucco house with his new wife, Ethel, who told Jimmy his father believed his son's return was "to sponge or freeload," unless he was willing to heed his father's advice.

It was a shame, Winton said, that Jimmy had been duped into thinking he could make a living "as some kind of an actor."

"It wasn't a manly profession," Winton told him, predicting Jimmy would find himself in a world of "pantywaists, dope fiends, drunks and queers" who would swiftly make Jimmy one of their own kind.

He'd thought it over, Winton said, and Santa Monica City College was the school Jimmy should attend, and study law. "Be a lawyer," Winton said. Starting out on the right foot toward a practical career was the answer. "You'll never learn to earn a living in a drama class with a bunch of sissies."

It was impossible for the son to communicate to his father that they had different views on what he should do with his life. At first Jimmy decided to let it ride, believing he could change his father's mind in time for the fall enrollment at UCLA.

Summer was just starting and Jimmy was in a different world from the one he'd been in since that train ride back to Indiana.

Although Ethel tried to make him comfortable, Jimmy felt out of place. He did not like the woman his father had married and he found conversations with her strained. She'd criticize him, though putting it into her husband's words. It wasn't long before all three felt cramped, as Jimmy would later say, "like cats ready to jump on another's back at any moment." He spent as much time as possible away from the house to avoid the tensions that arose with each face-to-face encounter.

"I wandered around," he said. "Maybe that's where the wandering around started.... I didn't have a bike then, but later I'd ride. Just ride. It wasn't where I was heading that was important, but just the ride, or the walk, from where I'd been to where I'd wind up...."

He'd find himself drifting through Santa Monica to the neighborhood where he'd lived as a child with his mother. "The movement of time can be a betrayer," Jimmy said. "T.S. Eliot wrote about it in one of his poems. Time betrayed memory because my father wasn't in the picture I'd carried in my head of what life had been like as a kid."

He'd walk to the library where his mother used to take him, and to the little park where they'd played in the sand. He remembered the touch of her hands, and if he closed his eyes he'd feel her lips on his face. He could feel her warmth flowing through him, as though the heat came from somewhere inside her—down through her arm and hand into his own.

Sitting in the little park with the sun beating on him, Jimmy felt a surging inside of himself that made him throb with pain, a loneliness sweeping over him with such throbbing force that he struck his fists against his legs. He clenched his teeth so hard he thought they'd break into bits. The sensation was of hurt and pain, of his bones breaking slowly by torture—his legs in iron devices. Or gored by the bull in the preacher's movie, the horn jaggedly running into his groin to tear his insides out.

His father's face mirrored the pain Jimmy felt in himself, though Winton saw none of it. Jimmy didn't hate the woman who'd replaced his mother, but he couldn't stay in the same room with her without wondering why his mother was dead. He didn't want to hear his stepmother's "reports" on his father's displeasure with Jimmy's "lack of appreciation." Jimmy knew he'd have to get out of there soon.

He wandered the beaches looking for a friendly face, hung around the bowling alley or spent afternoons on the pier. "For a few days I played around with the idea of joining a carnival," he told me. A man named Frank Greenberg, then forty years old, "with a stomach that stuck out two feet from his backbone," ran a concession on the pier and invited Jimmy to work for him and maybe hook up to a carnival.

"But the territory was Midwest," Frank said, "and Dean said he didn't want to go there. He'd just come out here to attend school and study acting, and he showed newspaper clippings from the hick town in Indiana. I told him it was a big jump from there to Hollywood, but he said he had a picture of it in his head like a personal reminder, or a Saint Christopher medal you hang on the rearview mirror to protect you.

Dean believed he could get from "point A to point C without getting his feet wet in the middle," Frank said. "All he had to do was step over it. We sat around the pier watching guys cut fish and we'd smoke some reefers. He said he'd smoked pot in high school once, when they were riding a bus, and the driver kept asking, 'What's that interesting smell? What the heck *is* that?'

"I had a Prince Albert can of good Mexican weed and we smoked it and I bought him fish in the cafe. He liked chips, but hardly had any money and once asked about moving in with me, paying for the space he'd take up in the room, he said, measuring it with a ruler and figuring he'd pay for what he used. He'd be the guy in the *Marriage of Figaro*, he said. I said I didn't get it and he said, 'The opera.'

"I had a small room off the boardwalk and there was hardly enough room for a *hotplate* let alone another bed. He said he'd use a sleeping bag he'd roll up when he wasn't sleeping in it. But the bed I had in there took up almost the whole place and I was crowded myself, so that was the end of that matter.

"He was okay, wasn't bothered about it, and said he'd get a job in the movies and get a place up in Hollywood. I told him he was probably good-looking enough to make it but he'd have to grow a few inches to buck Robert Mitchum. He laughed about that and said being shorter than Mitchum hadn't hurt James Cagney any. He said he wanted to be an actor like Cagney…"

One day on the pier, Frank recalls, "Dean was shooting around with a tall blonde girl, a kid like himself, and he snuck over for a couple of reefers. He wanted to smoke them under the pier with this girl. I stuck them in an envelope and gave it to him and they ran off toward the boardwalk. They went down the side of the pier, heading underneath, and it was the last time I saw him that summer."

While trying to make himself scarce at his father's, Jimmy got involved with a small theater group and worked on sets for a summer production. When he wasn't dabbing paint or moving props, he hopped a bus to walk around the UCLA campus. On weekends he'd catch the streetcar to visit the Hollywood Cemetery across from Paramount Studios. He'd walk around looking at movie stars' graves and monuments, or hang around in Wallach's Music City on Sunset and Vine, listening to records in one of the glass booths. For what seemed like hours he'd play and replay the recording of John Barrymore's Hamlet. "A true masterpiece," he called it. "There isn't a single word or syllable that doesn't become alive with Barrymore's rendition...."

Jimmy would play Hamlet on the stage, he decided; it would be the one crystal-clear goal of his life. Someday he'd be in New York. He'd be Hamlet.

As part of the deal to enroll in Santa Monica City College, Winton bought Jimmy a used Chevy. Jimmy began his freshman year as a physical education major, while signing up for as many drama classes as he could. There was another reason he went along with the plan: Attending City College as an out-of-state student would enable him to establish residency to qualify for UCLA's in-state fees.

Eighteen and with none of his ideas clear, Jimmy told another student, Diane Hixon, that becoming successful was "only in the mechanics of it." That was the part he didn't know—how it came about technically. There was so much to learn and so many things he felt compelled to do. "All the rest of it I have," he said.

Toothy, willowy, a blonde homecoming queen taller than Jimmy, Diane was the only girl he approached during the first semester. She remembers Jimmy "devouring recordings of plays, he liked Edgar Allen Poe stories and he was always hunched over, quoting half-aloud scenes from *Hamlet*, or other plays and stories he'd listen to on records that were told in the first person. We'd dated and he called me up one night while I was eating dinner and quoted some passage out of *Moby Dick*. We were going out, but he couldn't drive his car very good. He'd just run it against the curb, and like he'd get out and sometimes just leave the door hanging open...."

A few times they drove to a drive-in on Wilshire where Jimmy complained about his father and stepmother. "He told me he had to make a change or he was going to have a nervous breakdown. I didn't think much about the breakdown, but he was really troubled over his situation at home."

Desperately needing advice and reassurance, Jimmy stayed at City College with the nagging thought that as long as he abided by someone else's desires he'd never be able to do what he wanted.

Soon his ability to compromise collapsed. The following year he left City College for UCLA. He also left his father's house to find a cheap room of his own. Sometime after he enrolled in the theater arts department at UCLA, he managed to get a part in the college production of *Macbeth*.

He appeared more confident now, determined, and hung around briefly with a fraternity group, though this proved to be another hopeless attempt to get along with others and go the "accepted way," as he was to say.

He told fellow student Bill Bast, who was soon to become his roommate, that he wasn't a "competitor." He'd later say, "You have to compromise parts of yourself to get along with a lot of people when you don't believe in what they're doing. You have to do a lot of ass-kissing which I'm not willing to do."

Macbeth was the only college play Jimmy was to appear in

while at UCLA. The school newspaper panned his performance as lacking maturity.

The period of time Jimmy bumbled around the UCLA campus until he finally wound up heading for New York is a kind of hazy collage, a sort of mosaic without a theme. People and places intersect; remembrances collide with fact and tales told so many decades later seem to break away from the rumored history of his collegiate life.

Clearly, though, he was in a hurry. Described differently at times by those he crossed paths with, some things seem constant: chaos, confusion, abrupt shifts in direction, and relationships dominated his struggles.

He'd wanted to attend UCLA so he could appear in plays. The rest of the time in his classes, he usually slouched in his seat and stared fixedly at whoever did the talking as though he did not hear what was being said.

"He was a dreamer," one roommate recalls. "More astutely, he was a dreamer who differentiated between the dream and what was real only in the achievements, that the one might lead to the other." And yet Jimmy demonstrated "such fierce determination that all of his other impulses seemed to be shut off."

He had no patience for trial and error; he was not opposed to it, he said, only that the process took too long. Since there was no way it could be speeded up, he told his roommate, he'd have to race through it himself.

A few professionals could see that he was ripe for something. His first real acting job was doing a Coca-Cola commercial. Producer Jerry Fairbanks had come out from New York to shoot the segment. He wanted "all-American kids" bopping around a jukebox, and then on a merry-go-round grabbing Cokes instead of rings.

"Jimmy was the most active of the group," Fairbanks

thought. "His demonstration was so right for what Coke wanted—the perfect, all-American, bubbly boy-next-door— that we made him the focal point for close-ups, and set the other actors revolving around him."

His focus had shifted from thinking about parts in plays at UCLA, to the world of professional acting and he was starting to make the rounds of Hollywood casting agents. He managed to land a few bit parts on radio shows, and soon was so intent on getting into movies that he stopped going to school. It wasn't so much that he dropped out than that he just didn't go back.

Shortly after the Coke commercial, producer Fairbanks called Jimmy back for an episode of *Father Patrick's TV Theater*. The part was that of Saint John the Baptist, and the telecast was set for Easter morning, 1951. Jimmy worked with professional actors Gene Lockhart, Roddy McDowall, Ruth Hussey, and Michael Ansara in the biblical story. Though his part was small, he nonetheless played it with trembling energy and a clear-voiced resonance, "like an old Jewish actor," he said. An agent named Isabelle Draesmer thought he showed "interesting potential," and was sending Jimmy on interviews.

But some idle months followed this appearance when it seemed nothing at all would happen. Money was scarce and meals were stretching further apart. On the way back from a drive toward Tijuana to watch a movie being shot, Jimmy and a roommate ran out of gas and had to leave the car at the roadside. They hitched back to Los Angeles to find themselves locked out of the room, their belongings held for nonpayment of rent.

He had to borrow clothes. He'd mooch gas money or bus fare. He had a variety of roommates, but always problems contrived by Jimmy broke up the arrangements when he felt that the situation wasn't really doing him much good.

During Jimmy's halfhearted stay at UCLA, roommate Bill Bast felt he could be unpredictable and scary. The friendship with Bast was momentary—a kind of latching-on—as if each person he encountered could be a rung on some ladder of opportunity. "Those big, innocent blue eyes would start looking lost," one friend later said; "and that shaking of his head as if not understanding a damn thing you're trying to get across."

Jimmy would say, "Man, you're *weird*, you're really weird. What are you *talking* about?"

Bast said Jimmy'd try to "give you the routine that it was a moot point as to who was using whom, but he was, maybe innately, a pretty fair master of the reverse-psychology technique.... So you'd go off and watch the friendship break up and you'd be wondering if you were an okay guy or not."

With borrowed clothes, borrowed money, even borrowed underwear, Jimmy started "hanging around where it'd do the most good," he said. Getting dressed up one night in a suit that maybe needed pressing, the tie dirty, he'd go on the Sunset Strip to Mocambo's or upstairs to the Interlude bar where the movie crowd hung out, and pretend to be waiting for someone.

He'd wait for someone to pick him up, and might be taken over to Bel Air to another's house for cocktails and dinner. "Jimmy Dean could make himself so ingratiating and so warm and beautiful-looking that you couldn't resist him," says Phil Carey, an actor. Tall, very thin, with a "John Carradine" sort of face, Carey let Jimmy sleep on his couch several times.

"People gave him money, enough to tide him over," Carey says. "I'd try to get him to tell me what he'd been doing—to what extent he'd reciprocate with these different people—they were all gay people. He really didn't want anyone to know about it—his hanging around these predominantly gay social scenes. It was like something he'd been talked into, but would plug himself into when he was down, maybe just to be cared about, and carried, for a while. What I did get him to admit was that he was *passive*, or so he said. What he meant by 'passive' I wasn't sure—except to say he *acted* in a certain way expected by people, to get what he wanted. Which wasn't so hard to believe—he later proved to everyone his whole talent was in his acting. He came to life on the movie screen and left everyone else gray and far behind."

But Jimmy could be "nastier than hell at times," remembers another ex-UCLA friend. "I had a 'forty-eight Buick convertible and we'd head down to the beach.... There were other people he'd been friends with, and one was this fellow from school, his name was Kelsey, and the girl he was going with was in the acting classes they had.... she was going for a degree in it I believe— and Jimmy got into a fight once with Kelsey over the girl. She'd made up some story about Jimmy and her, which wasn't true, and it got back to Kelsey. They had an argument, but the important part of the story is that a week or so later we were down there by the pier at this cafe and the girl was there—Jimmy got outside with her, and they started arguing and I saw her slap him or shove him, and that was when Jimmy let her have it. He just popped her one, and she went out like a light, out cold on the floor."

Jimmy would not talk about it, and later when asked what happened and why had he'd laid her out, it was as though Jimmy simply did not hear the question, as though he did not hear what was being said. A few people thought he had a hearing problem.

"He seemed satisfied with himself," the actor friend recalls, "like he'd gotten a lot out of his system. See, he sometimes acted nasty when he drank. We drank quite a bit down at the bar on Hollywood because the guy there who was gay always gave liquor to you if you looked the age even though you weren't—he wanted a lot of younger guys around the place.

There was always money floating about, always someone to buy you something to eat if you just played along a little, and there was the possibility that you'd meet someone who knew someone who could do you some good. Like I know two guys who got through to Henry Willson. Next thing I know, one of them's under contract and in a picture at Universal.

"Most of the kids I was with were from broken homes or busted-up somehow along that line—and with no one you're close to, L.A.'s a mighty cold, cold, empty town."

5.

Making It Up the Ladder

Jimmy called Diane Hixon and asked for a loan to get a small room on Las Palmas north of Sunset Boulevard. Diane didn't recall how much she loaned him, but he got the room, then moved out after a couple of days, taking the sheets off the bed and the pillow with him.

Diane wasn't the only girl or boy Jimmy dug out of his college phone book, a tattered mess of loose cards and papers held between the covers of a Woolworth's secretarial folder. While at UCLA, he'd been seeing young Beverly Wills, an actress on CBS's *Junior Miss*, and the daughter of comedienne Joan Davis. Beverly had originally been dating Bill Bast. After she had gone out with Jimmy almost steadily for a while, she told her best friend, actress Karen Sharpe, "I must be going out of my mind to be seeing this person. I need a psychiatrist or something. He's the worst-mannered and rudest person I've ever dated…. He can be an absolutely cute guy and turn around and be a fucking asshole."

Karen Sharpe remembered a party in Hollywood near Bronson Canyon where Jimmy "apparently had too little to eat and too much to drink. "A few of us were out by the pool, though it was cold and the pool was empty which made the whole thing seem so much more dangerous and really surrealistic."

"Jimmy was reciting *Hamlet*, Karen says. "No one had been paying any attention to him and he was acting up. He walked out on the diving board and was emoting like a Shakespearean actor—not the 'To be or not to be' speech, but one of the other soliloquies. People were looking at him, wondering if he was going to fall off the board and down into the empty pool and break his neck. He started dancing on the tip of the board, and doing a pirouette so the board was bouncing up and down from the vibration.

"He'd seen the actor Anthony Quinn arriving at the party and then Quinn was standing in the doorway with a drink— these French doors that opened to the pool area—and he was watching. You couldn't *help* hearing Jimmy—he was that loud; his head back and looking up into the sky as he acted this out with all the flowing tones and that jazz.

"After a few minutes, Quinn asked, 'Who the hell's that?' I said, 'His name's Jimmy Dean.' Quinn grunted and said, 'You ought to keep a leash on him.'"

About this time, Jimmy had hauled over his sheets and pillow to bed down on the sofa at a CBS usher's apartment, "The guy's wife was out of town," Jimmy later said. This friend introduced Jimmy to an agent who became convinced that he should be sent out as a "pretty boy." This was based on an interview he'd had at Columbia. A taller actor got the part and the casting director said to Jimmy, "You're too pretty. We need a regular guy like a young Dane Clark, and you're too fragile-looking."

Isabel Draesmer reminded Jimmy there was no way she

could know how the studio was breaking down parts for casting directors, or who'd be right for any specific smaller parts. Nor could she know in advance of the general interviews that might be needed except "some young actors for this-and-that picture.... Any part you can get was the right part, and no one in the world can foresee when that might happen."

This advice, too, went over Jimmy's head because he was still certain he'd be successful in a short period of time. "He had his mind made up," she said. If a casting director or producer or screenwriter happened to dangle the possibility of a role before him, Jimmy was ready to desert anyone or whatever he was doing to climb up what he considered to be another rung on the ladder.

Eager to be acknowledged by these professional people and accepted into their ranks, Jimmy played the puppet for them; he was sure by then that the "political answer," Jimmy said, "being this one's buddy, kissing ass here and there—being seen in the right places, kissing the right asses"— that was the way to put himself across. Which to some seemed nothing more than an insatiable desire to see his name in lights and to read about himself in movie magazines.

Not, however, Phil Carey, still a movie extra living in a small apartment north of Hollywood. Carey knew a few successful actors, among them Stuart Whitman and Audie Murphy. And he'd met Lana Turner on a picture and knew the agent Henry Willson. He suggested a better course than the one Jimmy was on.

Jimmy would walk up to Hollywood and meet Carey in a little coffee shop near La Brea, a quaint old place from the twenties called C.C. Brown's. After a while Carey introduced him to various people he thought could help him more than most of the other people he was running around with. "He was letting himself be used but he was receiving little of any consequence in return," Carey says. His confidence had been drained and he was beginning to float. "Jimmy said he had one foot on that treadmill and the other going nowhere."

He did have some television film of himself, and through Carey he learned to pad his credentials to make more out of it than the film alone could do. What the studios were interested in, Carey told him, were "stars—they want to discover stars."

But Jimmy would take off his glasses and squint miserably through most of the interviews, peering across desks at casting agents and directors, offering a kind of unfocused gaze that had some saying, "The kid's on reefers."

He told Carey he thought "a lot of them" disliked him personally. "It's going to take a little longer, " he said "I know, it's going to be a little harder...."

Carey made a suggestion: "You have this fixation that you're already a great actor—a star, like it's a spiritual fait accompli! Only nobody else knows about it—"

"They don't know about it *yet*!" Jimmy interjected.

"Maybe that's what they need to see." Carey said. "Show them this positive picture you carry of yourself. It's got a lot of power. You know how many 'you's' are running around right this minute? Unless you hit them where where it means something, they can't remember you from any of the others."

He didn't "give a shit," Carey says. "There was only one person in the world as far as he was concerned, and that was himself."

Bill Bast was attending acting classes in Hollywood given by the actor James Whitmore, who liked to tell his prospective students that he'd refused to buckle down to Hollywood. He considered himself "an actor's actor," he said. He told Bast "Bring your friend by, let him watch a class. I'd like to talk to him."

Jimmy and Bill had given the roomate business another try.

A break in an all-day publicity shoot on Warners backlot. The "star" was being born.

Bill would claim years later that while he was gay, he had never shared anything physical with Jimmy. In fact, he said, he didn't really *like* very much about Jimmy, but believed his friend had to focus his energies and nervousness into something or he'd drive himself and everyone around him crazy.

Bill persuaded Jimmy to take Whitmore's class, but in a short time it became apparent that Jimmy was uncomfortable being criticized by the others. "Fuck you," he'd tell them. He particularly hated criticism from Whitmore.

"Jimmy would cringe as soon as he'd finish a scene," Whitmore said, "knowing he'd now have to explain himself to the rest of us."

Whitmore was aware of Jimmy's intensity but also what seemed an "obvious neurotic strain in the personality," he said. The class thought Jimmy downright rude—insolent, and not as special as he was giving himself credit for. One girl said, "He made me so nervous to trying to read a scene with him. He wouldn't pay attention to what the other person is doing. He was completely just into himself." Jimmy soon stopped attending. As he'd done with UCLA, he finally just didn't show up.

Again splitting up with Bill Bast, Jimmy became like "a teenage hobo," according to Karen Sharpe. "He'd gotten it into his head that he wanted to be like Marlon Brando, a difficult, rebellious person. I told him Brando had a lot of fame from New York—he'd been a success on Broadway in *A Streetcar Named Desire*. I said, 'Brando can afford to act like a jerk, but you're trying to survive—you're trying to get an acting job just to buy a hamburger tomorrow.'"

"He was so beaten-down looking," says a Los Angeles realtor who was an aspiring actor in the early 1950's. "Jimmy was all the mixed-up misfits he started playing on television a little later. He used to stand around with a hangdog look or he'd be walking around the area eating a hot dog and you'd think he was just looking for action. He used to walk up and down the beach strip, too, where the gay bars were. We'd drink beer and he said he had a great disappointment in Hollywood. Not because it hadn't discovered him, he said he wasn't that stupid. But he was sick of trying to make something happen, and if he couldn't make it on his talent, he didn't think he was going to make it at all. He said he'd jump off the end of the fucking pier."

Recalling how he felt as a nobody in Hollywood, Jimmy said, "You won't believe how I used to walk around and try to see these people, I mean the ones that had the position and the ones that were doing the casting, and I knew there were parts being cast that I was perfect for.

"It was really going on around me all the time and, man, I'd stop somewhere like in the windows of that Coffee Dan's on Vine Street because that was across the street from NBC and I was always trying to get something over there, if it was only a little part, and I didn't care what it was, but there were times I looked at myself in the window and I looked weird, man, weird…. It was like I wasn't real anymore, and here I was this kind of kid going around, but Hollywood was coming up over me—" When he said that, he made a building-up motion with his hands as if piling sand onto his head.

"Once when that shitcar wasn't running, I had blood in my socks because I got blisters from walking around all over there—no matter how much I'd go around and see these people it wasn't going to happen for me and I got lost. Simple as that—I got lost."

On one occasion he went two days without eating and with nowhere to spend the night. He crawled into a car in the NBC parking lot to sleep. Early the next morning the owner of the car was disturbed to find this young man curled up in the front seat. "He was a nice guy," said Jimmy. "He gave me some change and dropped me off where I was heading…."

The discomforts of being broke were short-lived, however. It didn't have to be a parked car; soon enough it was someone's apartment in Hollywood or a beach house in Malibu. "Jimmy wasn't destined to struggle for long," said Karen Sharpe. This was something so firmly believed in that it hardly mattered to him whether he missed meals or not.

Hanging around the Hollywood parking lot of the Brown Derby on Vine Street, Jimmy met Warren Dunn, a young television producer. Dunn's reputation in the Hollywood gay show business circle was well known; the scene that Jimmy later referred to as the "revolving meat rack."

Through Dunn, Jimmy met radio director Rogers Brackett at a party in the Hollywood hills, attended by Liberace, Rock

Hudson, and several others. Brackett, Jimmy was told, had been using young actors on a radio show, and was a remarkably influential fellow.

Brackett instantly beamed at the bemused Jimmy, and said, "You must be an actor. Nobody can look like you and not be an actor." Nodding, Jimmy turned on the charm, and Brackett said, "Why don't we have lunch this week?" Jimmy said, "How 'bout tomorrow?"

"Here was Jimmy," says Phil Carey, "the boyish farmboy when it suited him, and Rogers Brackett—older, suave, *trés chic* and influential." Brackett had been raised in the movie business as an extra, lived in an apartment above the Sunset Strip, and was notoriously gay. The "cowboy walk" (some say Brackett cultivated it and he claimed it was not an affectation) was what Jimmy later described as "sweeping the room without touching the floor."

That was how Jimmy's road to fame became paved, says Phil Carey. "Old Rogers got dazzled over Jimmy. The lunch no doubt turned into dinner and the dinner turned into breakfast and before you knew it, Jimmy was on a couple of radio shows Brackett directed. He was also hooked up with a big advertising agency out of the East Coast, but around town he was always buzzing right in the center of the gay clique that was a beehive from Hollywood to Malibu to New York City."

"It was basically a 'skin circuit,' says Carey. "These queens'd trade off tricks—take 'em to parties and pass them off to some agent or director or whoever happened to be there, and then they'd start looking around for another trick someone else was passing off—getting them out of their hair and making room for some new ones...." One well-known television actor told Carey, "I can't have the same person twice. I find someone and that's it—one night. Anything else and they want you to get them into the movies."

Brackett hadn't planned on getting *involved* with someone.

Carey says, "He told the screenwriter Leonard Spigelgass in Malibu that 'this one,' as he called Jimmy, was *special*. This one had talent and intelligence, only old Rogers confessed to Spigelgass that he was sometimes afraid of 'this one.' He said Jimmy frightened him occasionally with his 'unruly attitudes,' making Rogers wary and uneasy—like he'd brought something into his house not quite domesticated." Rogers Brackett was going to do all he could to try to get Jimmy obligated "to the hilt," so he wouldn't turn around and walk out when he had what he wanted.

Spigelgass wasn't impressed with Jimmy. The screenwriter said, "He was an ill-mannered, boorish young fellow and a great deal sharper than he allowed to be seen beneath the 'Aw, shucks' country-boy facade..." Another of the circle, a costume designer, said he couldn't see what Brackett was making such a fuss over—bending over backward to get "this one" into the movies.

A couple of years later Jimmy said to me, "I remember the first time I had to get the makeup on. I sat there and the makeup guy said, 'Put your head back and keep your chin up,' and he slapped it on and I knew then, squinting at the mirror, where and what I was supposed to be. But maybe I smoked too much or maybe I was drinking too much coffee but I felt sick sure enough, and I thought I'd puke all over the set—but that would've been okay. I was playing a soldier—I was sick and I was scared." Director Sam Fuller made *Fixed Bayonets* for Twentieth Century Fox, and though Jimmy was disappointed that he was no more than "a muddy army face in the background," he was now a working actor in Hollywood—a *professional*. His dream was becoming a reality.

Years later, Sam Fuller remembered "eager-beaver Dean." Fuller says, "He had something like only one line in the picture, but the reason he stood out in my mind is that I liked him because he was all bristling with excitement. He had incredible energy that was welling up in him and he was literally brimming over.... It was trembling through his pores.

"He wanted to talk to me and look through the camera," Fuller says. "I let him do it when we were setting another shot. He thanked me very politely and asked if he looked all right. "'All right?' I said. 'What do you mean?' He was in combat gear. He asked if he looked like he was in the midst of battle— through the camera. I said sure he did. He said he was glad— he *felt* in the midst of battle. I said, 'Well, take it easy and relax.' He wasn't up for a couple hours maybe. 'Go get a cup of coffee. Grab a smoke,' I told him.

"He thanked me again. And when we wrapped that day, he came over and said he was sorry he hadn't had a bigger part in the picture because he'd enjoyed working with me so much. He was the damnedest guy."

Outside the studios, Jimmy was constantly on the move. He'd stop by Phil Carey's, "as though to prove to me he was making the grade. He'd moved up into Rogers Brackett's apartment up above the Strip, and I said, 'How's it like living with Rogers?'

"Jimmy grinned and said, 'It doesn't hurt.' I said, 'How long you going to be shacking up with him?' And Jimmy said, 'Until it starts to hurt.'"

Carey ran into Jimmy a while later outside Sy Devor's Men's Shop on Vine. "He'd just charged a sharp pair of loafers—to Brackett's account, no doubt, and he came over for a while to smoke some pot and listen to jazz records. He told me he was seeing a lot of people—reading for a lot of parts in pictures and maybe soon he wouldn't have any need to be padding around these sissies."

It was all politics, Jimmy tried to tell Carey. "Getting work, he said, "is a matter of social politics."

"I said, 'Sure, sure, Jimmy. Politics and something else

they got a name for that isn't so political.'"

Again Jimmy grinned.

"He didn't take any offense to my needling him about it," Carey says.

The next picture he worked in was *Sailor Beware*, a Dean Martin and Jerry Lewis comedy. But the few lines Jimmy had were cut during the final edit. Yet people were coming through for him, he believed.

Not long after the Paramount job, Rogers Brackett maneuvered Jimmy into a five-day stint in a picture at Universal, later released as *Has Anybody Seen My Gal?* The movie starred Rock Hudson and Piper Laurie, and featured Charles Coburn.

During his week on the set, Jimmy tried to absorb as much as he could; even tried to get close enough to talk to director Douglas Sirk, but his part was so small they did not get together. Jimmy admired the director from a distance, and also told Rogers Brackett he sensed some sort of barrier around Rock Hudson—a number one boy in the business— like an invisible no-trespassing sign. "Not that he wasn't an okay guy in some respects," Jimmy said. "But they had him protected, watching every move he made." Jimmy later felt that this was only because the picture was pushing ahead on a close deadline and most members of the cast were edgy and impatient.

Also in the picture was Gigi Perreau, whom Jimmy managed to talk to. She said she was impressed with his naturalness, but offered that he should press ahead to get as much experience as possible. Working in television, she said, especially live television, was the same as going onstage.

Jimmy said, "But all the good television's coming out of New York. I'd have to go to New York to get work in those shows."

Yes, Gigi Perreau said. That was true. If an actor was dedicated enough to his craft, he should probably go to New York.

He'd heard it before. A lot of people were saying New York was the only way to get back into Hollywood. You made it first in New York—Hollywood would come looking for you. If you waited on Hollywood's doorstep to be discovered, you'd more than likely starve to death.

6.

Hitting Broadway

With Rogers Brackett footing the bill, Jimmy made it to New York via a roundabout trail. In time, James Whitmore would take credit for goosing Jimmy eastward, the only route to becoming a serious actor, and for having advised him—but not for financing his trip. Later, Warner Brothers studios would concoct a somewhat convincing (unless you knew the facts), fantasy-for-the-fans tale of a young man's journey to fame.

A number of people would vow not to talk about Jimmy after his death. They'd refuse to grant interviews. The carefully mapped blueprint for caution, supporting the manufactured tale, was intended to circumvent the involvement of Rogers Brackett in Jimmy's life, and to hide Jimmy's frequent forays in Hollywood's homosexual demimonde. The studio feared such revelations would sour the box-office returns of the two pictures Jimmy starred in, as yet unreleased at his death.

. . .

Rogers Brackett relocated to Chicago for the advertising firm, and took Jimmy with him for a brief stay until Jimmy traveled on to New York. As protective padding against hard knocks he was bound to encounter, he came armed with the names and numbers of several of Rogers Bracketts' friends who were hospitable. One was composer Alex Wilder, then living at the Algonquin Hotel, who arranged a room for Jimmy at the Iroquis next door. The older composer began to show the young man the town.

Another friend Rogers Brackett had recommended was television director Ralph Levy, then in Hollywood. In turn, Levy advised Jimmy to call on James Sheldon when he got to New York. Levy had worked at CBS in the East with Sheldon before transferring to the West Coast. Sheldon was then living on East Fortieth Street and working for an advertising firm while hoping to begin directing. He had already directed *We The People* for CBS, and a musical with Don Ameche.

"Jimmy was quick and eager," Sheldon says, "and he was very hungry to make a mark for himself. It would be awhile before I'd be able to actually help him by casting him in something, but I did send him to see an agent I knew—Jane Deacy."

Jimmy had a desire to fill himself with New York, Sheldon felt. "I think the city thrilled him completely; captivated him.... I was married and lived with my wife, and when Jimmy and I talked, he gave me the feeling that he was trying to get himself out of some situation which he said was like 'webs crawling' on him. He had very little money to spend and I didn't know where he was getting what he had. I loaned him some a couple of times when he said he hadn't eaten. But he was beginning to be a pest.... I had to try to get him working so he'd stay out of my hair."

One of the first television roles Jimmy did was for director

James Sheldon, with Gilmore in Santa Fe, New Mexico (present).

Stuart Rosenberg, who later made *Cool Hand Luke* with Paul Newman. "The show was a *Big Story* [episode]," Rosenberg said. Dean was rather noncommunicative, showing up in old blue jeans and a checkered shirt, and he had a pair of leather gloves hanging out of his back pocket. The show was shot on location and Jimmy spent most of his time sleeping in the bus or reading *Woody Woodpecker* comic books. He'd slouch in his seat and his eyes would travel across the pages of *Woody Woodpecker* even while someone was talking to him.

"He'd been so right for the part," Rosenberg says, "then here was this strange guy—like someone else had walked in after the part had been cast, someone else showing up to take Dean's part." Rosenberg, one of television's more sensitive and intuitive directors, recalls how it took him "maybe half the morning" before he realized that instead Dean might have stepped right out of the prepared screenplay. "When he got in front of the camera, it was an extension of his getting out of the bus and looking up from *Woody Woodpecker*, and yet it was so right."

In another show, Dean worked with veteran actor James Barton. Though Barton tried to help him, Jimmy wanted to be left alone by the other members of the cast. An actress on the show remembers that "Mr. Barton—who was a most generous person and had always helped others and especially the newer people—took it very much the wrong way. Dean's attitude was peculiar. He seemed nervous and his acting was highly strung, much more so than what his part called for."

Jimmy would "grin as he came into an office, wobbling his head up and down, keeping time to unheard music like a real 'hep cat,' which is what he was," remembers Barry Shrode, a production assistant for the live network shows of the period. "Always ready to break down and bust some law or something, some sort of trouble that no one understood and no one knew who to blame for.

"'What's happening, man?' he'd say, always this Negro jive talk. I don't know why he'd use that. I don't know what he was trying to say with it.

"He'd be on an interview or doing a show, and me, I'd want to hear what he'd been up to—I was always ribbing him about who he was in bed with. I was really partial to him, even to his sourpuss manner, those black shadows he gave off—but he'd grin and it was a lot of fun."

Agent Jane Deacy vowed she'd never talk about Jimmy after his death (a vow made also by the West Coast agent, Dick Clayton, who was to handle Jimmy in Hollywood through Famous Artists). She did let it be known that even though Jimmy slouched and looked moody and mumbled his words, he possessed a "bright, bright personality that he could switch on like a big lightbulb." He needed money in the worst way, and he let her know that he'd settle for any work she could get him—in the business. Would he be interested in helping out on a quiz show?

"Just you name it," he told Jane.

The show Jimmy went to work on was *Beat the Clock*. He was hired as a standby comic, and his job was to act out the sight gags and the comedy material for the prospective contestants, the things they'd perform (they were supposedly unrehearsed) during the show.

He'd also have to leap up and down like a monkey, scratching himself in order to break the stage fright and nervousness of the contestants, before the program. Soon enough he was telling people there was so much more that he wanted. He was always talking "theater" to anyone who would listen to him—plays and acting and Montgomery Clift and Marlon Brando.

The New York drama world was undergoing a change brought about by the stunning success of "Broadway's bad boy," Brando. Jimmy knew Brando's first film, *The Men*, released the year before, followed that summer by the movie version of Tennessee Williams' *A Streetcar Named Desire*, — directed by Elia Kazan, who'd also directed Brando in the Broadway production.

Brando had appeared at a propetious time. His abilities, like Montgomery Clift's (and like James Dean's to follow), were innate, learned from no source other than himself. According to Kazan, Brando had a "whole array of emotions to draw upon," a vast and varied field of sensations and conflicting emotions. Whereas Jimmy, he would later say, had "this one hurt," a kind of storehouse loaded with a single emotion, a deep hurt embedded and struggling within him. "It was what made people want to mother him," Kazan says, "that made the girls and boys and the faggots want to put their arms around him and tell him it was okay, that he'd be all right after all, that they would take care of him, guard him, protect him."

"There're some truly talented, beautiful people you can't resist," says Shrode, "who are instinctively able to captivate. Jimmy was one of them. Those who found fault with the way he went about doing it, were the ones who were perpetrating the false values that the kid was unknowingly cutting through."

Soon enough he was looking to free himself from the "obligations" that had been imposed upon him—reluctant to continue the friendships he'd had on the Coast. He didn't want to know "the Hollywood people" anymore. He was after a "New York life," he said. He was going to be a New York actor with another life for himself—making it by himself. There was no real room for anyone else. Or was there?

He'd wound up at the uptown East Side YMCA when he met pianist Frank Sheridan's daughter Elizabeth, called "Dizzy" by her friends.

She was studying dance, working part-time and living at the Rehearsal Club—a slim girl with long dark hair and an "exotic princess kind of face," as Jimmy later described her to me.

Men were not allowed in the rooms, but the girls could sit with guests in the evenings in the parlor until eleven o'clock. Dizzy was reading a magazine, and Jimmy was on an opposite couch—reading a magazine and waiting for a girl who was actually standing him up because she didn't want to loan him any money. "We started talking," Dizzy says. "He'd planned to eat something with the girl, who I knew. He said he was getting hungry and I said I hadn't had anything to eat and was pretty hungry myself."

He told Dizzy the only problem was that he didn't have the extra money for a snack. If Dizzy had any extra money, he said, they could probably eat something, though he was sorry he didn't have enough to take Dizzy to dinner. He was sure the lack of funds had sent the other girl on a date with someone else. "I've got enough for a couple of beers," he told Dizzy.

She asked him to wait while she went upstairs to scrounge up enough for dinner in case he was really as broke as he claimed.

"When I came downstairs he was standing at the front entrance, his back to the lobby, and looking at the street. I came to him and said I'd found some change, and he said to

Dizzy Sheridan in New York 1953, "Loving Jimmy—living with Jimmy... playing *La Bohème.*"

look how the rain was falling against the street at such a slanted angle. We stood there maybe five minutes looking at the rain and then he said, 'Yeah, okay, you got some change? How much you got?'"

She asked if he had an idea of someplace to go, and he said "What about Jerry's? It's an Italian joint around the corner."

They walked in the rain and Dizzy slipped—he grabbed her arm and then held her hand to steady her. He didn't let loose of her hand until they got to Jerry's.

"We were laughing because we were wet, like a couple of starving dogs coming in out of the downpour." Decades later, Dizzy would remember the red-and-white-checkered tablecloths and the warm atmosphere in Jerry's. Remembering, too, how it was to be sitting with Jimmy—who she didn't even know—in that corner booth, watching the rain through the window. "Neither one of us said anything right away but there wasn't any sort of strain in the communication. Even being quiet it was like we were talking—without words. I was thinking that it was like I'd been very alone in the world just a few minutes before we'd started talking in the club lobby. I'd had the feeling of being by myself and really wanting to talk to someone. Wanting to share things with someone—I don't know, thoughts, feelings.... even singing the words to a song together.

"When we did talk, everything he said seemed to hint at the idea that he'd felt the same way—incredibly alone in the city. Oh, even though he knew some people and things, but it was like he had nothing to connect to. He said he felt like something being blown around by the wind...."

So began the *La Bohème* romance of Jimmy and Dizzy Sheridan. He felt he'd seized hold of some sort of anchor, telling her he had a "friend or two," but he didn't really have anyone he was close to.

In a short time, Jimmy would say she was the only person

he felt close to. And he sang the song, "There Wasn't Anyone Till You...."

"Do you suppose it's possible to love someone," he asked Dizzy, "even though you don't know anything *about* that person?" Dizzy said yes. She believed that could be true. Together they'd go places and fool around in the park. They'd go to art movies in the Village and sit in cafeterias until the sun came up—talking. Talking. She felt they shared the same thoughts—maybe the same mind, his and hers somehow merging together and moving around and over the other as though like some split-apart Siamese twins but with the connection still there. "It was a matter of our spirits," Dizzy says.

Pooling resources, they rented a single apartment. "We'd spent so much time together it was dumb to be paying rents on two places. That's how we looked at it. But it was more than that. We wanted to be living together....sharing a life together because we'd fallen in love with one another."

Finances were tough. Jimmy had a bad cold one weekend and coughed so hard he couldn't sleep. Dizzy went to a delicatessen and "borrowed" two cans of chicken broth from an older lady working there. "She felt sorry for me and after a couple weeks I went back and paid her for the soup. But I had thoughts of maybe swiping it if I couldn't borrow it—things were that bad at one point. Actually the money was bad a lot of the time...."

She even convinced Jimmy to stop smoking that Sunday to give his lungs a rest. "He was laying there and looking at me as I fed him chicken soup from the pan, on a spoon he'd swiped from a Horn and Hardart cafeteria, and he asked me if I'd ever thought about getting married to someone."

"Sure," she answered. "If I think about getting married it's going to be to *some*one...."

They both laughed, and then Jimmy said, "You suppose it could be to *some*one like me?"

"What about you?" she asked. "When you think about getting married, do you think it could be to someone like me?"

That's how it went. "Later," Dizzy says, "Jimmy said maybe we should think about that sometime—he meant about getting married. 'Living with you,' he said, 'is like being married.' He said it was like we were married and living a regular life together. 'Like we're doing right now,' he said."

They'd listen to records on Dizzy's Webcor phonograph and she'd practice dancing in the small room. "We listened to opera and dramatic readings, and sometimes we'd just lay on the bed listening to jazz. To blues.... to rhythm-and-blues on 45's," she recalls, "and we'd make love and then swear our love for one another...."

For a short time it was like there was just the two of them. One morning Jimmy seemed very pensive and said, "Let's get married, Dizzy. Do you want to get married? I'm thinking about being married to you. Don't you think it would be all right?"

Maybe they could've done it right then, Dizzy says, "but one always thinks about tomorrow and you make plans for tomorrow." She couldn't see that Jimmy's tomorrows were bunched into his todays. He wanted to get married *that* day. That's what he'd been driving at.

He felt as if he'd grabbed a gold ring in a merry-go-round. He'd wangled himself out of the relationship with Rogers Brackett, who was still creeping around the edges of Jimmy's life, nagging him—calling him night and day, waving filets mignons instead of the Kraft cheese on toast—that Dizzy and Jimmy were sharing.

"He said he'd eat cornflakes with me instead of mutton with Rogers," Dizzy says. "He wanted me to meet this man, and when I did I got a kind of leaden, scared feeling in my stomach. Rogers was a creepy man, no matter what these people who knew him say. The first time I met him I'd gone over to Rogers' apartment with Jimmy. I felt it was a set-up sort of situation—by that I mean Rogers made it clear, if not by words certainly by intentions, that he had staked a claim on Jimmy. In his mind Jimmy somehow belonged to him and belonged in that creepy world the man lived in."

But Dizzy had also staked a claim, at least in her heart, but she erected no boundaries around Jimmy. "Rogers, on the other hand," Dizzy says, "had this whole set of rules and regulations for Jimmy. He'd remind him of how to behave and Jimmy'd just laugh at it, and in a way that seemed like he was laughing at Rogers, and maybe he was and that would infuriate the man. He was really like an old woman—he even looked sort of like an old woman made-up to look like a man."

And then Dizzy and Jimmy ran out of money.

"We had to vacate the little apartment. I got some money from my folks and from a part-time job, and I rented a room on Eighth Avenue. It was so small the door wouldn't open all the way because the bed was in there, and it was only a little single bed at that, like on an iron frame that was clunky and couldn't be moved around.

"We practically froze. Jimmy had that bullfight cape that we'd use on top of the blanket, but it smelled like blood—like a dead animal or something. It was a sickening smell. Maybe it was in my mind—the blood on the cape. He'd talked about the bullfights so much and how that cape had been used in the ring and never washed because it was some kind of sacred thing—like the love we felt for one another."

He went to stay with Rogers. Now that they had separate places again, even though Jimmy would come by and sleep over, Dizzy wondered where their relationship was headed. He'd nag about getting married. She couldn't figure it out. Did she *want* to get married? People were sort of doing it— "You'd pair off, but it was like sharing your pain." Was it because anyone was happy?

She began to question herself about her feelings for Jimmy—two years younger than herself, drenched with self-involvement that became more apparent the longer they were together. "He had an ego that couldn't be shaken," she says. Why couldn't he shake it? He had it rooted in *need*, "as deep as you could go." Yet she believed she was in love with him.

He had to make a success of himself and what was even harder to grasp was that he *knew* he would make it. "He said it was fated," Dizzy remembers.

He'd talk about Fatima—a fat Gypsy whore, he'd say. Moondog, a blind Greenwich Village character dressed like a Norseman, had the answers. Fuck everybody; cut a blanket over your head, stand around with a tin cup for handouts. You called your own shots. Fuck the rest of the world. Fuck the squares and the fat numb people that thought they had the answers. They didn't know shit.

Soon Jimmy borrowed money and rented another room at the Iroquois Hotel." It was larger than Dizzy's and she'd spend several nights with Jimmy in the hotel. "The bed was creaky and bounced around," she says, "like it was up on a bunch of metal springs."

Jimmy seemed troubled, "sad that we'd left behind the apartment," Dizzy says, "and the candles we'd light, and it was like he was talking about some other city we'd lived in. Some other life he'd had that was so distant, so far away from him...."

Busy with Rogers, with interviews, and with socializing with Rogers' friends, Jimmy came to Dizzy's room and said it made him sick to be around those people, "kissing ass with these assholes," he said. But he was making important con- tacts and he'd be working in another show very soon. He said, "James Sheldon's going to use me in a good show—he's a great director!"

Dizzy says Jimmy would cling to her in bed, "all bunched up in my arms, and it was like I was rocking him to sleep—like it was going to be painful for him to get up in the morning and have to face another day having to do what he was doing…." He didn't tell Dizzy exactly what he was doing, but within weeks he was working.

At odd hours of the night or day Jimmy'd frequently come "popping in" to ask Dizzy how much she loved him. Did she *really* love him? He wasn't talking about getting another apartment together. He was asking would she still love him even if they *weren't* living together?

"It was like I was a little slow to get the picture," Dizzy says. "Maybe having been so close to him like we'd been… It was in the back of my mind to ask him if he still wanted to marry me—if that's what he still thought about. But that would seem like I was pushing him. I never pushed him." She would eventually see that the reason their relationship lasted was because she did not "fence him in." Jimmy told Dizzy he'd talked to Rogers. "He said they'd had a long talk about finances, and Jimmy had mentioned the bad finances and the living situation, and Rogers suggested Jimmy stay over at his place. That way, Jimmy wouldn't have to worry about rent and he could put some bucks away until he saved up enough. Dizzy could do the same, and then, if they still wanted, they could combine their resources and get a "really livable place." A place where they could invite influential friends over for dinner.

"Like Rogers?" Dizzy asked.

"Well, what about him?" Jimmy said. "You think the idea of my staying at his place for a while is okay?"

Dizzy says, "What Jimmy meant was would it okay for *us*—for him to be there and me to be someplace else. Could we still be seeing each other the way we'd been."

Whether she felt it would or not wouldn't have made any difference, for in that moment Dizzy was opened to a complicated sort of experience that was actually the deeper nature of Jimmy. She saw that she'd never have him wholly. What'd she'd had with the candles and the chicken soup was perhaps the closest she'd come to a real life with Jimmy. A chill ran through her. She felt as though she was "sliding on ice," skidding on the surface of something while knowing there's a whole other life going on underneath.

Jimmy didn't want to live with Rogers. He wanted to live with Dizzy. But he was afraid he couldn't make enough money and they'd get kicked out again. He couldn't count on what she'd make, and that wasn't a fair situation. He'd hole up, he said, get some work and stash away some money—shooting all the while for a Broadway play. That was the *real* life for Jimmy and neither man nor woman nor beast could get between that sliding surface and all that abundance underneath.

Packing his only piece of luggage, a kind of canvas army bag with a hole in the bottom, Jimmy left the Iroquois when the week's rent ran out, and hotfooted it to Rogers Brackett.

7.

Changing Partners

66 **W**hat you had in your gut," said actor Billy Gunn, "was the qualification to push you over the top. If you didn't know it in your guts, you weren't going anywhere. Jimmy was right."

Out of every thousand there was *one*. "Jimmy knew he was the one, man, and it didn't matter what anyone else said."

"Don't ask me how he knew," Dizzy says, "but it was always there and in the way of everything we'd do. I had hopes— maybe call them expectations—in my heart about what sort of relationship I was looking for. I'd wanted to get involved and Jimmy'd been about as ripe as anyone for someone to pay attention to him. He was one of the loneliest people I've ever known."

Later on, none of the homosexuals who were part of the "showbiz scene" sympathized with Jimmy's severing ties to Rogers Brackett in favor of a kooky New York female dancer.

Jimmy said, "It's a course I'd set, you see, and that's what pissed them off so much—that it wasn't something that'd been dictated out of that 'regulations book' of how one's supposed to live and stay in the good graces of the cocktail crowd."

But the dilemma wasn't whether to desert Rogers in favor of Dizzy Sheridan, nor was it a question of Jimmy dumping the girl for the sake of opportunities offered by Rogers. Jimmy believed he would be able to have the best of both worlds, though he knew it wouldn't be easy.

He'd scoffed at the mother-hen behavior of Rogers as he had with Bill Bast's "nagging and endless platitudes." But Jimmy said, "To get to someplace as the crow flies you got to pass over a lot of crummy territory...."

Rogers later claimed he tried to train and tame James Dean, embroidering upon his relationship with him, fantasizing Jimmy's feelings for him.

"It was basically a case of wishful thinking," recalls Carlton Hale, one of Brackett's associates. "What you had was the silly—and hopeless—dream of the unfulfilled lover. Like praying the whore will awake to love you back. Not that Dean was a whore, though that rumor was generated right out of Rogers' circle. To someone like Rogers, a miserable—a basically miserable human being—if one can't love you back, then that one's unlovable. That sort of reasoning. A typically bitchy, homosexual rationale for that time frame. One *never* loves you the way you dream of being loved back....

"The rumor of James Dean as an ex-hustler for its own sake and wandering around for pickups is total nonsense," according to Hale, "as much a fabrication as actresses coming forth after all these decades and claiming they had affairs with Dean. The hustling nonsense started right here in New York, and was picked up by any number of people and writers eager to climb on the bandwagon. Because Dean took what was offered and left nothing behind, put a lot of frost on others...

"To get even, Rogers waited a long time—a miserably long time considering the waves he might've stirred back then by something like *Confidential* magazine or any of the sleaze rags—so Rogers stepped up to claim credit for much of Jimmy's success, and enlisted, let's say, the support of some of the other old queens—friends of Rogers'—to put it out that Dean's stardom was somehow a direct result of Rogers' beneficence.

"It's a case of the jockey taking credit for the horse—the radio taking credit for the music being played....

"Rogers babied Jimmy, who desperately needed babying, and sucked his cock and fell in love.

"Clearly, Rogers was helpful and instructive and somehow desperately wanted to manipulate that incredible raw, bold person behind the gentler facade Jimmy was so capable of exercising—when necessary...."

Rogers helped Jimmy, as it were, to conceal some of his anger—the intensity of his own confused feelings that brewed and churned even when he was sitting absolutely still. "In some ways, by holding that back beneath some proverbial 'silk suit on the monkey,' he may have done Dean a great disservice in the long run—and in the *short* run, as it were."

When Bill Bast showed up in New York, Jimmy suggested he room at the Iroquois. To Bast's surprise, Jimmy moved in with him after a short time, claiming that his roommate—Rogers—was giving up his apartment.

It was Dizzy's idea that the three of them take over the apartment of a friend of hers, on West Forty-fifth Street. "Bill can have his own bedroom," Dizzy said.

"It was fun being back with Jimmy but it wasn't the same," Dizzy says. "Bill was a very odd person—very possessive and fussy; he'd sleep in the other room with a lot of blankets covering himself while Jimmy and I would sleep in the other bed in the living room, and we'd lie there making fun of Bill."

Dizzy was working as an usherette at the Paris Theater across from the Plaza Hotel. "Just before Bill arrived in New York, Jimmy would stop in the theater often for coffee and doughnuts, which we served downstairs during intermissions." He'd told Dizzy how he was going away on a boat— sailing up the river with a producer, Lemuel Ayers, and his wife, both friends of Rogers Brackett.

Lemuel Ayers, producer and designer of the upcoming play *See The Jaguar* was close friends with Alec Wilder, who was composing the incidental music for the play. Though many actors were being considered for the part that Jimmy would finally be cast in, Jimmy expressed his confidence to Dizzy that he had the part.

"How can you be so sure?" Bast wanted to know, and Jimmy again talked about "Fatima," saying, "I gotta be faithful to her." Grinning, he mentioned "fates"—that things were predestined. "In any case," he told Dizzy, "it's predestined that I'm going to make it and that I'm going to make it like Marlon did, and I'm going to be a star."

Because of Dizzy's dancing, Jimmy enrolled into a class with Eartha Kitt. One afternoon after class, Eartha recalls, "Several of us were going uptown to see some rumba dancers at this club. Jamie—which is what I called Jimmy—wanted to talk to me after class and I said, 'I'm sorry, I'm going up to the club. Why don't you meet me up there?' I was going to meet this gentleman, a Broadway musical director, a really fine man, elderly. A marvelous man. So Jamie said he'd meet me there. I met the gentleman and we were dancing, and then sitting at his table and being very sociable, and all of a sudden Jamie shows up and says, 'Here I am!' and the old man just looks at him. I said, 'Oh, this is a friend of mine, this is Jamie Dean.' The next thing I know the two of them were getting into an argument.

"And it seems that ever since then, Jamie was sort of in my life. I began to teach him to beat the drums. We went to a few parties and I would be in the corner playing the bongos.

"We'd walk together, too. He was always there at the last minute to say come for a walk, whether it was raining or the sun was shining or whatever it was, and we would just walk, stop in some sidewalk cafe and get a coffee or a beer, go up to the dance studio which was on Forty-seventh between Broadway and Seventh, sit around up there and watch the other kids dancing for a while, and just walk around. And talk, constantly."

See The Jaguar was soon going into production, and Jimmy spent several weekends at the Ayerses' house, north of Manhattan on the Hudson River. He was asked to join the Ayerses' on their boat for a cruise. Jimmy quickly asked Dizzy and Bill to "hold the fort down," while he went for the cruise aboard the Ayerses' boat.

Later, unconfirmed rumors spread that Jimmy got the part because he granted sexual favors to Lem Ayers, but another story countered the rumors: Ayers had not wanted Jimmy for the part in *See the Jaguar*, but the playwright, N. Richard Nash, had insisted that "only James Dean can play it—he'll be magical."

Jimmy never said what happened between him and Lem Ayers or why he was aboard the boat, but few persons in the know doubted that some relationship developed between Jimmy and Ayers. As soon as he returned to town, Jimmy told Eartha that he had the part pretty well sewed up.

"I'll have to read for it," he said, "give an audition in the fall…" when the play would in fact go into production. "But it's only a formality," he said.

"I remember we went for a long walk in Central Park," Eartha says, "along the edge of the park, and out of the blue he said that his mother would be proud of him. He was actually going to be on Broadway in a show. Nothing had been announced yet about the cast, and it seemed that the reading he'd have to give was only for the sake of others to appear that he'd gotten the part by genuinely auditioning—not that he'd landed it by spending days on a boat with the play's gay producer."

Eartha claims that after that day Jimmy began to bait her about her own childhood. "It had to do with articles he'd read. Usually any articles he'd read on me, he'd ask me about them and find out whether they were true. Now he was trying to tie them in with his own family story...."

It was difficult at times to tell if Jimmy was telling the truth or not. He'd been asked about his biography—for the play—and he began to piece one together in the manner Brando had done—coming up with some outrageous but interesting lies.

"Jamie felt he was a loner," Eartha says. "He was all by himself, there was nobody, really. He was still living with that girl who was also a dancer and that character from the coast—" The three of them always made Eartha think of the Three Stooges.

"He said we were a lot alike, Jamie and myself, and he gave me the impression that if anything was to happen to him I'd be there—he said that I would be there. I was like that sister that he'd missed."

When Jimmy knew his part in the Broadway play was secured, he broke off his relationship with Rogers. But The Three Stooges stayed glued togther in the cramped apartment. "Bill would keep the door closed tight between the room he had and ours," Dizzy says, "sometimes putting a bunch of towels or dirty laundry down over the crack at the bottom of the door... Jimmy and I would snuggle in bed, cuddling up, and we'd laugh about Bill—it was like living with an old woman, for god's sake. He couldn't stop fussing and putting in his two cents where it wasn't wanted. Jimmy grew to resent him quickly, and so did I. He was, frankly, a damned pain in the neck."

Since slipping out from beneath Rogers' wing Jimmy was having hard financial times. He'd call Rogers, ask for a loan, but Rogers would tell him he had to come back over—bring his "gear" back over before he'd be able to help him. Rogers felt, Dizzy believes, that anything he might do for Jimmy would somehow benefit me—or even Bill—and that was something Rogers wasn't about to do. "In fact, when I'd see him" Dizzy says, "he'd look at me like he wished I'd fall over dead."

Dizzy held the job at the Paris Theater movie house, now being visited by both Jimmy *and* Bill for the free doughnuts, while Jimmy was making the rounds of casting offices. Jimmy often couldn't sleep, she recalls. "He couldn't explain it, or wouldn't explain it…. Sometimes he'd just walk out—wouldn't say where he was going—wouldn't tell us when he was coming back."

He'd wander around at night, he told Eartha; hang out in twenty-four-hour diners or go to Forty-second Street movies to fantasize acting the roles on screen.

To get out of the city for a few days, Jimmy, Bill, and Dizzy hitchhiked to Fairmount, Indiana, for "some good home cooking," as Jimmy put it.

However pleasurable the trip seemed for Dizzy and Bill, it was quickly regretted by Jimmy for reasons he wouldn't share except to later complain that he'd been "betrayed by those two." Going back to Fairmount proved a "psychological catastrophe."

While pooling resources back in New York, after the trip to Fairmount, conflicts more closely tied to personalities than scanty income soon soured the situation. Dizzy believes Bill was frightened of Jimmy's "bad boy" tricks while he was involved in the play, and her own coziness with Jimmy was becoming a "second fiddle situation." "Jimmy said he'd do almost anything to get ahead," Dizzy says, "and I wasn't the one to stand in his way or impose what I thought of what he was intending to do."

Dizzy felt that "fate" came bumping into their lives and set "things kiltering off in other directions. Not only for Jimmy—for all of us somehow. I had the chance to go to the Virgin Islands to dance. I'd be gone a long time. I wanted to get going—moving my career ahead as well. I almost felt as drawn to doing that as Jimmy did to his acting—to chasing television jobs. I say 'almost' because I still cared for him more than I felt he cared for me. He wasn't going to budge one foot across the threshold and get into my life."

She saw her relationship with Jimmy as "visits" with a bird that would land on her windowsill. "This wonderful creature that would come to me on its own terms to be loved and taken care of. But if I didn't watch myself it'd take wing and be gone."

On an evening radio show on the Sunday before *See the Jaguar* opened, Jimmy discussed a book—on Aztec civilization.

He told the interviewer, Jack Shafer, that he'd "always been fascinated by the Aztec Indians. They were a very fatalistic people, and I sometimes share that feeling." He continued in a similar vein, in the following manner: "They had such a weird sense of doom that when the warlike Spaniards arrived in Mexico, a lot of the Aztecs just gave up, fatalistically, to an event they believed couldn't be avoided."

"Like Kismet?" Shafer asked. "What is written, is written?"

"See, for them," said Jimmy, "the arrival of the Spaniards was written. They had a legend that their god Quetzalcoatl had predicted they would be conquered by strange visitors from another land."

"Well," Shafer said, "no wonder they were fatalistic about

it, then. But what's all this about your being fatalistic, too?"

Jimmy said, "In a certain sense I am. I don't exactly know how to explain it. Things happen to us—we simply attract our own fate. What I mean is we make our own destiny."

"Doesn't it bother you, that sort of thinking?" asked Shafer.

"Not a bit," said Jimmy. "I think I'm like the Aztecs in that respect, too. With their sense of doom, they tried to get the most out of life while life was good, and I go along with them on that philosophy. I don't mean the 'Eat, drink and be merry, for tomorrow we die' idea, but something a lot deeper and more valuable.

"I want to live as intensely as I can. What I want to do is enjoy the good life while it is good. And that's how those Aztecs felt. They were a happy people, very hospitable, generous to one another, and extremely fond of beauty and music."

Though Jimmy often voiced his daydreams about the "happiness of the Aztecs," he also delighted that those same Indians believed that it was suffering that was the real god-pleaser, and that through "pain of the spirit" one could control fate. The Aztecs were certain that the only way to escape the everlasting misery of life on earth was to be killed in battle or to have one's heart cut out on a sacrificial altar. Then you could be free.

"Suffering is good," Jimmy told Dizzy. "Suffering is the only way to understand what you're all about." On another occasion, as if to prove the point, he once bent apart a big safety pin and pushed the sharp end through the top of his thumb. He held it up, examined it carefully, then pulled the pin back through his skin. "You see?" he said, and smiled.

See the Jaguar opened at the Cort Theater on December 3, 1952, and proved a great personal success for Jimmy.

Walter Kerr, in the *New York Herald Tribune* reported that

Dean "adds an extraordinary performance in an almost impossible role"—that of a bewildered lad who has been shut off from a vicious world by an overzealous mother, "and who is coming upon both the beauty and the brutality of the mountain for the first time...."

Jimmy was the "toast of the town," says Dizzy, who was invited to the cast party at Sardi's restaurant following opening night. What she observed was a "different" person than she'd known. "This was a different James Dean, emerging right out of the person I'd been so closely involved with."

The play, which had received poor reviews, closed after only six performances, and Dizzy says, "Jimmy seemed to disappear after that. He wasn't around—he didn't call. We all just went separate ways, more or less.... I couldn't reach him because I'd leave messages at the phone service Hayes Registry and he wouldn't answer them. When I did see him—a few times— he said he was very busy with interviews and a lot of television work that was coming up. But what disturbed me was his distant manner. He was almost cold— very aloof."

Jimmy was putting Dizzy at arm's length, afraid that she'd bring up the subject that he'd wanted to get married—and now that was something he wouldn't even consider. He wanted to forget about it, but he couldn't tell her that.

Jimmy never seriously thought of Dizzy as "overfreight" or excess baggage. Several months after we met, he told me she'd run off to the West Indies "to dance in some kind of tin-pan band." He gave me to understand that Dizzy had deserted him by going away, and leaving him "broken and sad."

Dizzy says, "He made it clear it was finished. He didn't even want to talk about how we'd lived together. He was finished with Rogers as well—*really* finished with him, and he was washing his hands of Bill."

It was as though Jimmy was shedding his skin and everything

that had been attached to him in some way had to peel off and drop to the ground as well. Dizzy soon left the country for the Virgin Islands, to work as a dancer.

Jimmy was like a trickster who carries cards and can make one pop up at the right moment. "It was intuitive," Eartha says, "and geared along by a kind of inner ideal as to what he had to do with himself." And in the end, what most thought about his relationships with roommates, friends, with the few girls he tried to get close to, was that some idealistic guideline prompted him to give a little of what they sought, while he made all the substantial gains.

"Because of his personality and because of his good looks—though being an attractive guy in itself doesn't do it— the way Jimmy Dean presented himself was such that, even before he really started to make it, he'd already built up a cult around him, already built up people who thought very highly of him...." So says actor Steve Ross, at the time rehearsing for the Actors' Studio production of Calder Willingham's *End as a Man*.

Ross says the early 1950's witnessed "the beginnings of a resurgence of the art community of the Village—there'd always been an artistic community there, but during the first few years of the fifties, more Off-Broadway plays were being done, art galleries opening up on Bleecker Street, more people coming downtown."

The Village crowd, according to Ross, sought artistic expression the equal of Geraldine Page's in Tennessee William's *Summer and Smoke* at the Circle in the Square, an Off-Broadway theatre. Another big influence of the day was Eugene O'Neill's *The Ice Man Cometh* with Jason Robards.

Jimmy Dean "was the sort of guy who, when he came on the scene, impressed a lot of young people in both the Village and the uptown scene," adds Ross. "He had an attitude that was not commercial, yet we were often surprised to hear [he] was going to be working in something because we never knew he was even looking for it.

"It was like a self-containment about him, with him saying, 'I got something and I want to preserve it and I want to make it work right for me but whatever happens— happens....'"

8.

Start of the Craziness

You had to have gone through the Hollywood rat race to appreciate what New York might offer an ambitious young actor bent on something more than sacking down with dubious producers, casting directors and asshole agents.

Ida Lupino had been a kind of mentor and advised my heading east for some honest theatrical experience. Actor John Hodiak, another mentor, suggested the same. I'd met Hodiak at MGM and he'd helped me get an agent and line up bit parts. Heading to New York himself to appear in a Broadway play, Hodiak recommended my taking a break from "celluloid city," as he called L.A.

It took me three days on the Greyhound bus to New York. One sole of my blue suede loafers came unstitched from hooking my foot on the rung of the seat in front, and flapped as I walked across the Pennsylvania Station depot, carrying a big blue Val-Pac and a smaller overnight duffel bag.

Another actor I knew, Charles Bronson, working steadily in smaller movie parts, told me to try the Sloan House YMCA when I got back East. "It's in the middle of town," he said, "and shouldn't cost much until you get a regular room or apartment somewhere else." He said a bulletin board at the YMCA usually had notices on rentals. "It's an okay place," Bronson said, "if you keep one hand over your crotch and the other on your wallet."

I walked along Thirty-fourth Street with my bags, surrounded by crowds in the bottom of a canyon. I couldn't see the sun and no sunlight reached the streets. People were moving quickly as though someone'd yelled, "Fire!" A guy was coming towards me but far to the right side—moving against the foot traffic and sort of creeping against the side of the buildings, falling as if he couldn't stay on his feet. He was dressed like a lawyer but had blood all over his face, and a stunned look. Nobody stopped to ask him what was wrong, they kept moving around him like ants do as they travel around one another.

A cop in a little coffee shop gave me some directions. I'd sat down next to him after a block or so, told him I was from L.A. where my dad was a cop. When I told the New York cop I was an actor, he paid for my coffee and doughnut and said, "Welcome to New York, kid."

It was muggy and steamy by the time I checked into the Sloan House, a huge building with an old, very big, clanking iron kind of elevator, like a huge cage with all the lines and pulleys exposed overhead.

The room was very small with an iron single cot, a chest of drawers, and a wardrobe cabinet that opened out. I hung my suits and vests and slacks—most of them tweeds that'd kill me in the heat. I looked out the little slot of a window and I couldn't see the street. Only a part of a bigger building to the west. The sky was gray. I wanted to get out and get going; I felt

I wasn't in the city yet. I wasn't in the picture I had in my mind and I had to get into New York right away.

I dressed up in a suit and walked around, heading to Times Square. It started to rain and I want under the awning of an orange-juice stand, drank some juice, then coffee, and smoked while I waited for the rain to let up. I was in New York—standing at the mouth of Times Square. It towered and flashed before me like a shimmering in the neon and mist and the movement of heat.

For a week, no matter where I went on interviews, I got lost. I didn't know the streets, which were cross streets or uptown or down-. I was at Thirty-ninth and Sixth Avenue and the way the streets branched out I didn't know which one would take me where I had to go.

The air in New York didn't smell like anywhere else and it was full of black soot. I got a big piece stuck on my eyeball and a guy in a drugstore took it out for me. We got to talking about New York and he gave me the address of an apartment on Forty-seventh he'd seen for rent. It was just past Eighth Avenue, west of the Biltmore Theater, and Ethel Berrymore, and the Strand, and on the same side of the street as the Mansfield Theater. I found myself living in the heart of the Times Square theater district.

Though I was yet to run into Jimmy Dean, I had also been friends with Warren Dunn in Hollywood. Through Warren, I met the producer of *A Streetcar Named Desire*, Irene Selznick, who took me under her wing for a while. She had produced *Bell, Book and Candle* on Broadway, by John Van Druten, who was convinced I was perfect for a part in a new play he was working on.

Irene arranged a number of appointments for me with producers and casting agents, and even connected me with a modeling agency. I was on a photo job in Astoria, Queens, when I passed a garage and saw an old Norton motorcycle with a For

We'd wonder around and he'd snap shots of me and other nuts on the streets of New York. Photo of the author by James Dean

Sale sign tied to one handgrip. An old guy without an arm said the bike had been left behind and they were selling it for storage and parking charges.

I paid for the bike over a couple weeks and rode it back to the city dressed to the teeth. At nights I'd chain it to a pipe in the small alley where the garbage cans were lined up.

Late one night not long after I'd met Jimmy, I'd been working on the lines for a play and had just dropped off when someone knocked on my door. I opened it, and Jimmy was standing there holding his greasy hands up in front of him. He seemed surprised that I'd been asleep, and said he'd been downstairs working on my motorcycle. He said my carburetor wasn't original and that someone had "jockeyed it around getting it on the engine. You do that?" he asked. I told him it was like that when I'd bought it.

"A bad idea," he said, "using spacers like that." A friend in Santa Monica had used a part that wasn't stock and the bike leaked gas. "Burned the bike up," Jimmy said. He asked if I'd ever rebuilt a carburetor for a Norton, and I said I hadn't. He said it wasn't hard, then asked if he could use the sink.

After washing his hands, he stood in the middle of the room looking around at the walls. He said, "Where's the bullfight pictures?"

I'd told him of the photographs, and he said he thought I'd have them all over the walls. When I brought out the box I kept them in, he got down on the floor and went through all of them, studying each one, even turning them sideways. We were still there when daylight came.

He found a picture of the matador we'd talked about and said, "Here it is!" and mumbled about men with mirror swords and eyes dripping blood; flowing capes and pinpoints of death in their pores. He said it was from a Mexican poem, but I imagined he'd thought it up right on the spot.

Again he wanted to talk about the matador I'd seen gored,

and again I told him what I remembered—the horn hooking and nailing the bullfighter. He said he was sorry I was just a bullfight fan and didn't think seriously about doing it myself. I took that as a joke, but he claimed that bullfighting was something he'd have to do someday—learn the cape and face a bull. "Maybe one about this size," he said, grinning, his hand held waist-high.

But he said he could see it—it was there, a speck in the back of his mind. He said it was a "black-burned hole in one of those old-time photographs…" It was like "getting married or dying," he said. "Your life opens up in that one moment, and that's when you're the most complete you can be…."

He wanted to borrow the photo to put on his wall, "as soon as I get a wall," he added. The truth was that he did have a wall—actually four, in a garret room in a five-story brownstone. He'd told no one about the place for fear they'd rent it out from under him when he ran out of money for the lease. The toilet was in the hall, no kitchen, and it would prove so small he'd keep his hot plate in the hallway.

Once, walking along Forty-second Street, looking at the whores and nuts and movie placards—one for Brando's *The Men*—Jimmy said he had a snapshot of Brando with a cock in his mouth. (However, the photograph he was talking about has never proven to be Brando.) He had another picture showing Brando in a room with a porthole window behind him. Jimmy said the shot had been taken in a room on West Sixty-eighth Street and, grinning, he said, "*I've* got the place—the same apartment." Someone he'd met through Marty Landau and who worked out at Terry Hunt's with Brando, had given Jimmy the address of the apartment in the Brando photo. Jimmy said he dogged the manager of the building until the place became vacant. He believed it was the same apartment, the same porthole window.

"By the way," he said, "I've found out that Brando's fucked

around with a couple of guys from Terry Hunt's, and one of them says Marlon keeps rolling over onto his stomach. So he loves taking it up the ass," Jimmy said, joking. He made a circle with his thumb and finger, and left saying he had a rehearsal in less than twenty minutes.

He'd seen a dead guy loaded into a paddy wagon and called me up because he said it'd troubled him so bad he couldn't sleep. The man's hand was sticking up as if reaching, he said, but it didn't move. He wanted me to walk around with him—over on the West Side and down along the edge of the river.

"What's on the edge of the river?" I asked. "Dirty water."

"I want to see what it's like," he said.

"You can get fucking killed over there," I said.

"You die, you die," he said. "You think you're going to die?"

"I'm thinking about staying alive," I said.

"But it's the thought of dying that makes you think about staying alive."

"Down on the river at night's some kind of risk I'd rather not take," I said.

"If you don't take the chance, you don't see what it's like. How do you know what's there? Maybe there's something you got to find out."

We walked past the Music Box theater and the Bijou, heading west. When we got to the Henry Hudson Parkway, we stared walking south. It was after midnight as we passed the Forty-second Street Ferry and stopped around Fortieth Street in a little dock cafe that had a small lighthouse structure on the roof. A kind of sinking fog was blowing in on the piers. He had a little bunched-up wax-paper ball he unwrapped and handed me a white pill. "Bite it in half," he said, "and swallow the rest of it later." I asked what it was. "Bennie," he said. "You can walk all fucking night, man. It opens up your eyeballs...." We gulped the pill halves and drank coffee, and he wanted to know what I thought about dying young. We were back on the dying subject. "Are you scared of dying?" he asked.

I said I didn't know. "I don't want to push it to find out if I'm scared or not."

"How old's your mom?" he asked.

"She's forty or forty-one," I said.

"My mother died before she was even thirty years old," he said. "She wasn't afraid of death. You know what scared her? Losing life—losing what she had."

"That's too bad," I said. I could feel the pill kicking my heart into third gear.

He said his feeling was that he couldn't stop her. That's what was too bad, he said. "I didn't want her to die. I didn't know she was dying—not exactly. Maybe a part of one knows—senses it in some way whether you're old enough to understand what's going on or not." That's when he told me he'd been nine years old when they'd buried her. "But she'd been sick for a long time. Getting sick—" he said, and laughed a little oddly. "It's like sinking off a pier. You want to reach that person and they're sort of calling up and they're sinking down but no matter what you think you want to do, they're gone." He said one goes into a darkness as black as the dirty river. "No matter what they say, there isn't any heaven. There's no hell, either." I asked him what he thought there was and he said, "There's nothing. There's nothing before you're born and there's nothing after you're dead."

I said, "If that's the case as you see it, what's the sense?"

"It's fear," he said, "that keeps you going. Fear of being nothing, and fear of having pain." He said, "There's nobody I know that isn't afraid of pain." He hadn't figured it out yet, he said, but he knew there was an answer in it somewhere. It was the kind of answer that kept eluding his search but it was something he was stuck on, and he figured it had something to do with his mother's death.

Once, a little foggy on beer in Jerry's Tavern, we talked about the childhood amnesia that was mentioned in a psychology book on interpersonal relations.

Lee Strasberg, the head of the Actors Studio, often quoted a particular shrink on how an actor recreating experience draws from the depths of his childhood. "So much is forgotten," Jimmy said, "because as little kids we're taught that our shit is something bad—it's foul and disgusting. Piss is bad." He said Strasberg had talked about the smell of a mother's body locked up in the child's memory. "He talked about the smell of a mother's breasts," Jimmy said. "We're taught to shift away from these close senses, smell and touch, like an animal's senses, and we're forced by convention to experience things through the distance senses—the eyes and the ears—what we hear...."

He could remember a lot about living in Santa Monica when he was little. And he remembered watching his mother wither away in pain. He said years later he hitchhiked to Marion and slept on her grave.

"I stayed there a day and a half," he said. "Slept there all night, and that day I wandered around looking at other graves and reading the headstones of the people buried there."

Often, I'd find Jimmy in a Horn and Hardart cafeteria or a greasy hamburger joint around the corner on Forty-sixth. He'd be nursing coffee and aching over things he had no power to change, or maybe picturing ways in his mind he'd be able to change the things he thought he couldn't.

Or he'd prowl the streets, often dropping in on people as if finding holes in the city in which to hide. He told me he had to know things—roll them into a ball so it was complete for him. "Or else what you're trying to get ahold of just disappears."

· · ·

Jimmy was obsessed by an idea, that of fusing all experiences into one intense moment. It was one of the ideas that nearly drove Eartha Kitt nuts. "He couldn't let go," she said later. He'd latched on to Eartha as a soul mate—nothing sexual between them. She told me, "We're like brother and sister." Jimmy was convinced Eartha had "special powers" and knowledge she could deliver to him by some kind of osmosis if he hung around long enough.

She had locked up in her "a sense of magic and the answers," he said. He'd badger her into long discussions, and while she enjoyed his friendship, she said at times it was almost painful for her—like when he'd devise some theory he knew she'd disagree with. "He'd play the devil's advocate— people had to get shook up. Sleepers had to wake up.... Painful arguments when you knew you were debating noth- ing—a phantom—an idea that slips through your fingers like water, leaving nothing."

He was inclined to learn a little, she said, then attempt to teach the instructor. If Eartha thought he was wrong about something, he'd insist she didn't understand what he was try- ing to say. "It was one-sided. Jimmy wanted me to prove to him or demonstrate how he wasn't right. He believed if I understood what he was trying to say, then I would agree with him." He had to meet with her at such times and try to make her understand.

For example, there was his theory of "synchronization." He sensed moments in Eartha's performances when it seemed to him that everything she knew was fused directly into the moment, even things having nothing to do with per- forming, he thought, translated directly into one energy force—a magic connection. This moment of fusion was "synchronization."

He phoned her one night to ask her to meet him at the

cafeteria. Jimmy had a small flask he used to spike the coffee, cup after cup, chain-smoking and sipping so intensely, she said, "He seemed to buzz with electricity…sparks flying off of him."

The flask held brandy. Marlon Brando, he said, drank hardly at all, but when he had to get to the meaning of something, he drank brandy. Jimmy wanted to learn and compress what he knew into one energy force representing "something perfect." He had to dance and sing, learn photography and bullfighting because he *knew* that what he'd learn could come through in some other way, would make up qualities he could project as an artist—as an actor.

She told him she understood. "But whether or not all that can be 'fused' into a whole, some performance or art as a single energy, I didn't know. My logic inclines to say it can't, because life doesn't operate on single notes. It's a whole symphony."

When she tried to tell him the "lessons of living" were orchestrated by God, Jimmy laughed.

"What bullshit!" he said. There was no God—there was only art, only the composer, the creator of the symphony.

"And God created him who creates the symphony," Eartha said. Jimmy laughed again. "He said I was passing the buck—shirking off and not taking credit for my own perfection. He said that was how people go around walking in pig crap all the time. He didn't think I understood or was using my real knowledge to get at the answers he needed."

"He wasn't playing in anyone else's symphony," Eartha said. "He was a loner—a solo player, and those meetings with him were excruciating and frustrating and trying…"

A few years later, photographer Roy Schatt, whom Jimmy had wanted to learn from, displayed portraits of Jimmy in Rienzie's, a West Fourth Street coffeehouse. The young actor had bugged him mercilessly. "He was a miserable runt who was a genius at posturing a different guise for almost everyone he came in contact with," Schatt said. "Alone and left alone, he was just that—miserable, a squinty-eyed runt. But he was like an electric bulb—you plug him in and there's all this light…. A battery or something inside the person generating this incredible light…. He wanted me to teach him everything about photography. I don't know why. I was the photographer. He was the subject, but he wanted to be as proficient as myself. I said, 'What for? All you're interested in is yourself!'"

Jimmy smiled at him and said, "Who else is going to be looking out for me?"

A few days later, Jimmy came to my apartment wanting to learn how to fence in an hour or two. I said it couldn't be done, but tried to show him how to hold a foil, as one would hold a bird, firmly but carefully. But he clutched at it, his moves sudden and jerky, and he couldn't bend one of his fingers. He was still in Eartha's body-movement class, and though she'd said the fencing was a good idea, Jimmy quickly lost interest in it. I didn't know why he'd wanted to learn.

We'd smoke cigarettes and drink coffee, meet or run into one another, and it got to be pretty much the same thing each time. He'd sit with one foot up on another chair and rock it on its two legs. Sometimes he wore an old pair of black English riding boots that had been cut down to cowboy-boot length, with the stitching coming apart and the sides of the heels all scuffed. For a long time he stared out at the rain beating on the sidewalk, or at the people hurrying back and forth past the doorway. Every so often he'd laugh and point out something that amused him, but then he'd slump back down and chew at the skin around his thumbnail.

I felt that whenever we had coffee or met to eat something

together, he'd kind of drift out of the world he was generally in and spend a little time getting his bearings—though not for long; and soon he'd have to pop back into that world and disappear again.

His staples were coffee and Pall Mall cigarettes, the latter puffed down to his fingers, then he'd use the burning butt to light another one. Sometimes he would talk about his throat. He worried, it seemed, a great deal about his throat, and whenever it was cold he'd keep a scarf wrapped around his neck.

Sometimes he'd drink beer and talk about people—personalities—Jean Cocteau and Edith Piaf; the amazing work of Jean-Louis Barrault, actors like John Hodiak and Tallulah Bankhead. I told Jimmy I'd met Edith Piaf at the Château Marmont in L.A. the year before, and I had her records.

About Bankhead, Jimmy said, "She's the superb prima donna bitch." He was fascinatd by her mouth, he said. It was a kind of living thing with a mind of its own, apart from her personality. It gave him a hard-on; he wanted to stick his dick in her mouth.

Sometimes he'd make a point of saying something funny to one of the waitresses. He'd say to her, "So you're not mad at me anymore?"

She'd reply, "No, why should I be mad at you?" I guessed her age at forty-five, maybe a little less. I thought Jimmy had something going for her, and in a short time she did, too. But when she became friendlier and more like a woman responding favorably to someone's approach, Jimmy started to back off, to make himself smaller at the counter, and then he stopped coming into the drugstore.

One night he was in a bar on Third Avenue, waiting for a waiter he'd met who worked in a little Village cafe. He told me the waiter slept on a slab door with a Japanese neckrest. Like Jimmy, he wore a motorcycle jacket and even black leather pants while hanging around the Third Avenue bar. "These weirdos are fucking and torturing each other," Jimmy said. "You got to see what these people are like, but the only way to do it is you gotta wear a bike jacket and boots, man. Are you game?" he asked me.

9.

Going for It

Jimmy told James Sheldon to whom he introduced me at the Armstrong Theater offices, that I was a "kid iconoclast," a Rimbaud on a beat-up motorcycle. Others would say, "He's one of Jimmy's people—art for art's sake." Jimmy's association with Actors Studio was minimal; and he was disliked by members of the board.

Lee Strasberg was a very ugly man, Jimmy said. "He keeps no mirrors in his house for fear of catching sight of his own reflection." Neither Montgomery Clift nor Brando were affiliated with the Studio, and Jimmy felt that it was unnecessary for a talent such as his own to be criticized by "the ugly man" who had a "personal vindictiveness" toward him, all the while favoring others who kowtowed to Strasberg's opinions—or who "fuck or suck off" the board members.

"Strasberg's ideas are nothing more than personal opinions," Jimmy said, held by Strasberg to be true, "and as Nietzsche puts it," Jimmy said, "it isn't that they *are* true, only that they're *held* as being true." And, Jimmy said, the instructor's opinions were "mostly hot air and hogshit." He mimicked Strasberg's self-importance, even the roundness of the man's bald head seemed to glint from Jimmy's impersonations. The voice was Strasberg's, mouthing silly, nonsensical statements or stodgy platitudes.

"He sits there in this posture, this ugly man who is married to an ugly woman," Jimmy said, "and farts out these opinions while half of the people in the place run around goosing each other."

An inability to take criticism had caused Jimmy's resentment of the Studio, according to John Stix, then head of the board. "Jimmy's self-indulgence wasn't tolerated by Strasberg, nor did he allow Jimmy to use it as a defense against criticism—so Jimmy disliked everyone in the Studio, except a couple of people like Kim Stanley and Geraldine Page who tended to allow more margin for his indulgences than did anyone else there..." Stix said that Jimmy's calling most of those connected with the Studio "a bunch of daisy-chain faggots" only seemed to hint at his personal confusions over his own sexual ambivalence.

Jimmy delighted in the few times I became sarcastic and blasphemous. He'd chuckle, and encourage me to get drunk and shoot my mouth off. James Sheldon said, "Dean aligns himself with the castigated.... Point someone out as a mainstream reject or someone so wounded in some way they have a terrible negative attitude—a creep, and Jimmy goes out of his way to get close to that person. In that way you'll be caught off-balance, never knowing who he'll show up with or what he'd do next."

There was always the angle of shock. Jimmy would stir up ridiculous situations to upset people. Once he suggested I dress up as a girl and we'd visit some people. "These flakes and some chicks'll be there," he said, and he'd introduce me as a girl he'd met, and we were "getting serious—going together." Then at the party he'd find out I was a guy. He'd be very upset and we'd fake a heated argument, but then we'd kiss and make up. The making up, he said, would "get them to the quick."

One day, rather off-handedly while we were talking about Actors Studio, Jimmy asked me, "You ever had something to do with a guy, or just fooling around?" All I'd told him at that time was that when I was fifteen I'd gone to a Hollywood party at the Garden of Allah, and Tyrone Power, who was drunk, squeezed my hand, patted me on the head, then kissed me and said I was the most beautiful boy he had seen in a long time. He wanted to kiss me again, trying to stick his tongue in my mouth but I kept pulling my head back. Since then I'd gotten regular propositions, but I'd never had an *affair* with a guy. I'd just been experimental and trying to get around.

Jimmy said the idea of us going to the party—me as a girl—was a "great idea," and we talked a little about people being bisexual. He said he didn't think there was any such thing. If someone really needed emotional support from a male, he would probably be homosexual, but if he needed the support from a woman, then he'd be more straight.

That season he hit a point in New York of deliberately shifting his relationships, dumping those that had been of help, for those he needed new help from—and breaking away from those people no longer tolerant of his "bad boy" pranks.

James Sheldon liked Jimmy, worked with him and helped him, but even Sheldon took a dim view of his behavior. "He's changing for the worse," Sheldon told me, "and he can't even see it…. He's becoming a son of a bitch, but damned, I'll still try to do what I can to see that he gets straightened out. The question is—what the hell does one do?"

In Jerry's Tavern one night, the subject came up of Jimmy having hitched rides to Indiana with Dizzy Sheridan and Bill

Bast. Jimmy was moody—impulsively phoning Eartha from the bar. He came back to the table to say he was a stranger to himself. "What you see before you is a human cockroach," he said. Around this time he said he was doing a dramatic reading of Franz Kafka's *The Metamorphosis*; whose hero awakens one morning to find himself transformed into a giant cockroach.

Skip Lowe, a young singer and actor, was at the table, and for Skip's sake Jimmy went into a tortuous monologue about how, like Thomas Wolfe, he couldn't go home again because he was no longer the person he'd left in Indiana. While he was showing the place to his "good friend" Bill and the "only girl for me," Dizzy, the two were picking apart his personality, "tinkering around with my brain." He kept saying to himself, "Hey, who's this person I'm looking at in this place that isn't his anymore?"

Eartha told him, "You could see yourself as the little person you used to be, but it wasn't you anymore." He was astonished that she understood what he'd gone through. "I'd been to that place in my own life," Eartha said, "and had to face the fact that how you'd lived since back then changes who you are."

He was afraid of that, Jimmy said. Eartha told him he was changing into the person he really was, that the other one had been the child. "I told him with those other people he had shared the child," she said, "not the person he was changing into."

Another time he asked if I had any marijuana. He wanted to get high and was sorry Curry wasn't around because he always had grass. But all I had was cheese and soda crackers and a quart of beer, which Jimmy drank quickly. He was restless and edgy, and seemed trapped in the space of the apartment. I'd been fooling around with a painting, a view from my window of the corner drugstore and the firehouse across the street. "There's no people in the picture," Jimmy said. I said

I hadn't painted any into it yet. He said if it was his painting he'd leave it empty.

I put on Alex North's music from *A Streetcar Named Desire*, but it only made him jumpy. He couldn't sit still, bracing and tensing his shoulders and squinting through his glasses at everything. At one point, staring at me, he said, "If you put on a wig and dress you could play a chick." He made several phone calls, drank the beer and made faces because he didn't like the taste of it. Did I have anything else to eat? he wanted to know—something like cake or cookies. I said I didn't but suggested going out somewhere.

"Like where?" he asked. He said he was starving. His belt was full of holes, he said. He was lying. James Dean rarely went without a meal in New York.

There was a pretty good French cafe on Ninth Avenue, but Jimmy said he didn't know much about French food, and he was broke to boot. He then said James Sheldon knew "all the French stuff," and had suggested dinner a couple of times. "Sheldon's got money," Jimmy said, and *he* could pay for the dinners.

He phoned Sheldon, who knew the restaurant and would be waiting in front for us. Our spirits lifted, Jimmy bounced down the stairs. But by the time we walked over there, his mood had changed again. He sat hunched at the table, guarded and suspicious of what Sheldon ordered. Once he tasted it, though, he dug in, wolfing the food down.

He soaked a crêpe with sweet syrup before eating it, almost floating it. Sheldon stared at him and said, "You're going to eat that?" Jimmy picked up the crêpe in his hand and squeezed it until the filling oozed out. He thought that was very funny. Sheldon said, "You're a knucklehead!" and rubbed Jimmy's head—one of those Dutch-uncle rubs. "This guy's a *knuckle*head."

Sheldon ordered another bottle of wine though he drank

little of it. However, embarrassed by our behavior, he paid the
check and left early. Jimmy though, wouldn't leave until he'd
eaten all the crêpes and bread, and finished the second bottle.

We were walking back toward 8th Avenue when he told me
he'd been in a show with actress Irene Vernon. They were eating somewhere when she complained about the greasy potatoes, "swimming in grease," she'd said. Jimmy thought that
was funny, but Irene was upset that the grease was spreading
to the other food. He removed the potatoes from her plate, he
said, and put them into a water glass where they could "swim
properly," then used a napkin to wipe up the grease from her
dish. She could spread the other parts of her meal, he told her,
onto the place where the potatoes had been.

Heading north again, we stopped at Jerry's Tavern, drank
beers and were smashed by the time we got to my place.
Because the conversation got around to sex with guys as well
as girls, I told him about an actor friend with whom I'd stayed
overnight at a country club. It surprised me, I told Jimmy,
when the actor showed me his cock, and how big he could get
it.

I wasn't sure what I thought about seeing him like that.
Jimmy wanted to know if I'd been in the sack with the producers I'd met, and I said no—except for a couple of them,
but I didn't like it. Something like with my relative—him
going down on me—though with my stepbrother he'd want
me to have sex with him by my doing it to him from behind.

"Buttfucking him," Jimmy said. I said yes, and Jimmy
asked me in a serious voice if I'd wanted to suck the actor's
cock, asking me almost like a doctor might ask when and
where I experienced some sort of pain. He said, "Be honest
with me, be as honest as all the days." What did I feel about
the guy's cock?—because it seems to stand out in my mind, he
said. He laughed at the unintended pun, and asked me how
come I didn't do it.

I told him the guy surprised me and I was scared. I couldn't say more about it than I already had.

Jimmy said it was probably possible for him to have a relationship with a guy, too, and to have a physical exchange without it being labeled "homosexual," because he felt something like that, like what the actor and I came close to, was like an extension of the friendship. "Just going to the edge of the friendship or sort of beyond it," Jimmy said. He didn't think any kind of sexual experience would push him or anyone else in one direction or the other.

He wanted to know if I had sucked my relative's cock, and I said I had done that once or twice. He'd have me shoot in his mouth, and then fuck him in the ass. Jimmy asked me about another producer kissing me, and I said I didn't like it.

"Have you tasted jizz?" Jimmy asked. Did I know what it tasted like? I said I tasted my own on my finger. I said, sure I know what it tastes like. Jimmy said, "You're like a little girl who puts her finger in her pussy and then licks it off her finger." Did I like the taste? he wanted to know.

We both laughed. No I said. I 'd spit it out. "Is that why you were scared of that guy's dick, because you didn't want to have that stuff in your mouth?" That was the question he was asking me. That's what he wanted to know.

I felt nervous. "I don't know.... What about you?"

He didn't answer, but began to giggle. "I am not active. I am passive.... You are passive from what you have said to me." But "active" and "passive" wasn't the same, depending on what a person happens to be doing, he said. With my relative I was being passive, but by fucking him I could be said to be active if it was what I *wanted* to do. He said it depended on how it all happened, and what the person wanted. "How it happens to come about," he said. Circumstances—the nature of the "interpersonal relationship," he said, were what was important.

He was lying on my bed with his head hanging over the edge, and I was sitting in the wicker basket chair. At one point I tried to get up but I was too drunk and ended up on the floor near Jimmy. I reached up and touched his head, then pulled on his hair. He said, "Man, you know more than just being kissed by Tyrone Power. You know things like I do 'cause you've been through the same shit."

We talked for a few minutes more. There was a strange sort of vibrating in the air, a kind of intimacy that was electric and exciting. He put his finger on my lower lip and started to giggle. Then he turned his head around and was sitting facing me. He put his hand behind my neck and pulled my face toward his, putting his lips on mine. It was the first time I had ever really been kissed by another guy. He said, "Come up on the bed before I break my neck." I moved alongside of him and he kissed me again. Our teeth touched, stuck together in a strange way. I closed my upper row of teeth down onto his lower row, so that I could almost bite his bottom teeth by closing my mouth. I felt his tongue against the edge of my upper teeth, and then I opened his lips and he put his tongue in my mouth, pushing it against my tongue. I put my hands up at the side of his face and we stayed like that for a few seconds until we backed up onto the bed. He kissed me on the neck, and bit—though not really hard—into the skin between my neck and collarbone, and then he was laying on top of me.

"Can you be fucked?" he asked.

"Jesus!" I said. "I don't think so."

He said, "I want to try to fuck you. We can try it if you want to." He wanted me to put my arms around him—which I felt funny doing—and to hold him. He wanted me to kiss him while he moved his lower body against me, and to keep kissing him. He wanted to suck my nipples. We tried to experience something more, some physical sort of thing. Again he bit me, and this time it felt sharp. He was holding himself and he said,

"Am I going to fuck you?"

I said I guess we could try. "I don't know how successful it will be...."

"We have to use something," he said. "You know what I mean—what've you got?"

Some skin lotion was all I had. I replaced his hand with my hand. I tried to go down on him but his cock was big and made me gag and choke. We tried to fuck but it didn't work exactly as we wanted it to. I lay on my side, sort of, and he lay against my back, one leg on mine that lay behind me. With the stuff, the body lotion, it was possible for him to enter into me a little ways, and as long as he didn't push hard into me it was okay.

I didn't know what we could do. It was like it wasn't going to work. Whatever the hell sparked such a situation between us was just going to be all bound up by the impossibility of the mechanics.

We stopped after a few minutes. He said he wanted to go into me farther, but I didn't think I could take it like that. He asked me to use the cream and to put it on his cock and rub it back and forth, fast but light, he said until I could feel the heat of the friction.

So what I was doing, jacking him off with the lotion. I kept pouring it on and working up and down and then he just sort of began to jerk and the stuff came up out of him—jumping kind of.

But we kept trying. This part of the friendship stayed in the background over the next few weeks, jumpy and spotty; we'd connect like electric wires and it made sparks.

It had to do with his being perverse about things, drawn, as if by a magnet, to what struck him as perverse. He'd tell me he saw me as a kind of teenage Rimbaud who didn't like anybody, and he liked that. I'd been told by others that I was misanthropic and that it was bad to have negative thoughts, but

Jimmy liked this. He was excited by it. He laughed about derogatory things he'd say about people, and he'd encourage me to say bad things about others, especially to their faces.

We were two bad boys, though not in the delinquent or criminal sense. That was how our relationship would develop— I encouraged whatever craziness he'd think up, and the physical side or attempts at it were extensions of the intensity of this relationship. Ours was a kind of affair between bad-boy spirits.

Like spontaneous combustion, we'd open ourselves to carnality and sort of explode into it—a fast, quick, rushing together. I'd jack him off and go down on him. He'd say, "Forget about trying to open your mouth—just let it open up. Your jaw won't hurt. I can go all the way into the back of your throat." After a short time, he'd say, "You want to do it again?"

He'd do the same, squatted on his knees between my legs and taking my lower body up to his mouth—my thighs at the sides of his ribs. For me, the physical thing was still awkward, but it was exciting and had a kind of burning-up sensation to it. I doubted that we got much satisfaction. Bad boys playing bad boys while opening up the bisexual sides of ourselves.

This dimension of our friendship occured almost apart from us and not much attention had to be paid to it. It was cerebral energy, a wonder or excitement, but still scared me. For Jimmy, the *idea* and the anticipation of coming together seemed more intriguing than whatever we actually did.

Caught up in our own ambitions, what we shared wasn't really an *affair* by far, nor was it what has been written about our friendship in books and magazines over the years. One book describes it as "salacious" and "lustful," but that isn't what it was exactly. It was rather a time of exploration, not so much physical as something else.

I'd run into him and there'd be an energy between us, even

in the company of others. One was a girl he was still seeing, Barbara, a young actress who I thought cared sincerely for Jimmy. I knew he really liked her. One night in Jerry's, we were joking around and drinking, Jimmy across from me in the booth, and for a second our eyes met and that look was there, but just for a second. If either one of us had been a girl, we'd have surely fallen in love, though it probably wouldn't have lasted.

10.

Discovery

arly in the fall of 1953, we went to a party on Forty-fifth Street around the corner from the Algonquin and the Iroquois. Jimmy'd done another show with James Sheldon who showed up briefly at the party. He'd moved to Gramercy Park South and was becoming one of New York's most active and creative television directors. But he said Jimmy and himself were momentarily at odds over the latter's attitude: The more work he got the more antagonism seemed to fly between Jimmy and those he worked with.

William Inge didn't want Jimmy in one of his plays because, he said, "His moods are so unpredictable and he scares the pants right off of me. What if he decides to tear the script right up in the middle of performance?"

Jimmy was wearing a pair of army fatigue pants he'd picked up earlier that week. We'd gone into the Army and Navy Store on Forty-second Street and I gave him some money, even though he had a wad of bills in his pocket. He'd said I owed it to him because he got me a job, through a photographer he knew, posing for a cover on a detective magazine. It was a photo of me as a teenager in a hot rod with a crook looming in the window, pointing a gun. The idea was that he was about to rape the girl I was with. She was terrified and cowering on the floorboards.

In the surplus store, he'd bitched about the price of a pair of fatigue pants with pockets on the lower legs, no back pockets, like Brando wore in *The Men*. Jimmy groaned and tried to squeeze the price on the marked-down sale tag. He told the guy, "They're for my *brother*, man, who's in a fucking *wheel*chair!"

We still had enough for the movie on Forty-second where he wanted to see *From Here To Eternity* again.

Jimmy said another photographer, Don Manfredi, would be at the party and could take pictures. I'd met Manfredi through Jimmy months earlier at a Nedick's orange-juice stand. He had a stack of photos he'd taken of Jimmy when Jimmy'd been in the play. "He's a real artist," Jimmy told me, "a painter and a great photographer." The party was in a studio above a manufacturing loft, a lot of people were there, and Jimmy was hiding in the kitchen. He'd reached up under the rear of my jacket, grabbed hold of the back of my pants and pulled me into the kitchen to conceal ourselves by the ice box.

Jimmy was stuffing his face with crackers and potato chips and some kind of cheese sauces he said tasted like shit. The wine was flowing and I was mixing it with soda water while Jimmy struggled to open a can of salmon with a bottle opener. At one point he hammered the can against the side of the sink. He wadded the salmon into his mouth. At that point some other people came into the kitchen—actress Betsy Palmer, who'd done a show with Jimmy; Billy Gunn, a young black actor, and a blonde, teenage-looking actress named Sharon Kingsley. When Jimmy saw them, he faked choking, making gagging noises with his mouth wide open and the salmon falling out.

Palmer made a terrible face and said, "I love you, Jimmy, but you're a master at becoming sickening."

"He was caught up in shocking people as Brando used to," says Billy Gunn. "Only with Brando it was like a game—a 'fuck you all' stunt he'd pull, like scratching his ass and picking his nose in front of you.

"It was hard to tell if Jimmy was actually serious, though— I mean if it was some sort of goofiness about him, you know, like maybe all the nuts and bolts weren't fastened down tight. I thought that before I knew him personally and then when I did, it was a different story. He became my hero."

Later, though, Billy complained because Jimmy didn't help pay for a bag of marijuana although he'd smoked his share. "He was very stingy—very tight about money back then, not that the money itself meant a lot to him, but what he did have he'd selfishly blow on himself."

That night Billy was rattling on about the Actors Studio and Geraldine Page, and about the play adaptation of André Gide's novel, *The Immoralist*. Jimmy nodded, playing dumb, not letting on that he'd landed a good role in the same show which was headed for Broadway. He pretended to know nothing about Geraldine Page starring in the play, along with Louis Jordan. Jimmy's part was that of a homosexual Arab houseboy, and Billy had been signed to understudy the same character.

Billy was bragging about getting the understudy, and Jimmy just said, "Oh, yeah?" and "What play's that? Who's in it?" The fact that Jimmy had signed for the role hadn't been announced, but he finally told Billy and said, "They're keeping it a secret in case they have to fire such an asshole as me before we get into rehearsals."

"That's okay with me," Billy said. "If they do, I'll go on in your place!"

He left the kitchen. Jimmy stared after him and said, "What a fucking *jerk*, man." But Gunn would become one of the few people Jimmy would be friendly with that winter— part of Jimmy's "uptown" group. Sharon Kingsley was still in the kitchen—she'd thought the salmon stunt was a riot. She was looking for some sort of mustard in the cabinet and found a bottle of licorice liquor. She popped the lid off and drank some down.

"Oh, this is good!" she said.

Jimmy said, "Who did you come here with?"

"Billy and Betsy," the blonde said.

Jimmy filled paper cups with the liquor and we swallowed that down until the bottle was empty. By then Jimmy had his arm draped around her shoulder and he kept edging her toward me, facing me with her handfuls of breasts inches from my chest. He asked Sharon if she wanted to go with us for a beer, "somewhere where we don't have to look at all these ugly faces—these ugly-faced, inconsiderate slobs. You want go have a party of our own someplace?" he asked. She laughed. Sure, why not? She said one party was as good as another; the only difference was the quality of the grog you'd be drinking.

"That's not the only difference," Jimmy said. "Good parties are where you're taking off your clothes.

Though he was still seeing Barbara, they fought like "cats" and she didn't know what she was looking for. Jimmy's advice: She should marry "some joker with fat lips and big thumbs…"

He'd keep his friends all pretty separate from one another. If two of us who knew him showed up in the same setting with him, he'd withdraw or start acting weird—pulling some kind of stunt.

That night we piled into a cab with Sharon between us, headed for Seventh Avenue South. In what seemed like moments though, she had her hand in his pants and he'd taken mine and buried it in her crotch.

When we reached Twenty-third, we had the driver turn and head back up into Times Square to my place on Forty-eighth. Jimmy played with her, urging her to take off her clothes and "show us" what she had.

She didn't mind any of it, but left on her brassiere and underpants until he'd fooled around with her some more and had the bra off. She was swinging her breasts, showing us how she could bounce them by muscle control and roll her stomach in and out.

She kept reaching for his cock or feeling his ass, but he seemed more intrigued by her behavior than involved with her sexual preoccupations.

I'd stacked several records on the player and by the time we were running thin, she was on the bed in the small bedroom and we were both rubbing her body with Nivea lotion, including her bare ass. Jimmy seemed very gentle, carefully making sure he had her skin covered with the lotion from her neck to her toes.

He said "The record's stopped," and I climbed off to turn them over. I could hear the bed creaking and when I got back on it he was in the midst of fucking her. He finished while I lay at her side, and when he got off of her, she turned a little to face me and reached her arm across towards my shoulder. I moved over on her and lay on her, kissing her, while Jimmy sat on the edge of the bed, his back to us, sort of hunched down a little at the middle.

After a little while, he said to Sharon, "Why don't you suck my cock?" and she sort of got down on the bed, her lower body curled against me. A lot of heat was coming from between her legs like she was on fire, and it felt like a radiator against the middle of me. It felt really good to be pressed into her, and while she was sucking Jimmy's cock, I pushed against her and in a moment her legs opened, one sort of scissoring back and on to me and I was between her legs. I pushed my cock into her and she groaned and laughed a little, making a muffled sound because Jimmy's cock was in her mouth.

Looking over her back and shoulder, I could see the underside of Jimmy's chin because his head was thrown back. She started moaning and gasping and her head was going up and down fast and it was like I could feel both of them shaking, both of them connected and shaking and it came right down into the center of her body.

One afternoon Jimmy introduced me to a Park Avenue art dealer named Fred Delius and joked about him looking "remarkably lifelike."

Jimmy had met him at a show he'd gone to with Leonard Rosenman, a musician friend, and Delius invited us to his gallery. Jimmy wanted to show me two works. One was an old Spanish painting of Saint Sebastian; the other was a portrait of Rimbaud "in drag," by a French symbolist painter.

From a smaller room with a table and chairs off the main gallery, you could look directly at the large painting—Saint Sebastian, almost life-size, bound to a tree with hands tied, his body pierced by arrows, head tilted back slightly with his eyes raised towards Heaven. Jimmy stayed trance-like in a chair, smoking and staring at the painting while Delius showed me his latest acquisition in another room. The *Rimbaud* he said, had been shipped to another gallery, but what he showed me was a peculiar work of the Virgin Mary holding the infant Christ.

The baby's face looked wrinkled and strained, its teeth like an old person's. The Virgin, I later told Jimmy, was how I imagined an embalmed Jean Harlow might've looked. As I stared at the painting in a kind of awe, I felt Delius's hand moving across my rump, and he tried to kiss the back of my neck. He whispered in some other language, and I moved away. He implored me to come back for dinner, and I said I'd let him know. As I walked away from him, he said weakly, "I can help you. I can be influential. You might ask Jimmy if I am not sincere."

Jimmy had dozed off, chin resting on the folds of his sweater which was spotted with cigarette ash. His eyelids were slightly open and the whites of his eyes were visible behind his glasses. He wasn't interested in the proposal Delius had made to me. "He's an old queen," Jimmy said. "He's okay and who gives a shit?" The dealer had wanted to fly him to Spain to see the bullfights. "Fat chance."

Restlessly, almost anxiously, Jimmy wanted to talk about the bulls again—the gorings and funerals of matadors. Then we turned to talking about how long it would take Saint Sebastian to die from those arrows in him. One sticking in his lower abdomen must've pierced organs, Jimmy said, and he had to be bleeding inside. "That'd kill him," he said with certainty. He talked about being hanged—and suffocation, and was trying to imagine being guillotined, and whether the eyes fluttered with any last-second sight.

The death talk went on—through several beers at a little place on Thirty-fourth by Herald Square. The subject of dying and dismemberment wasn't as exciting or interesting to me as it was to Jimmy. The discussion was never morose, though, and at times he'd tend to get almost ecstatic. Details became important and purposeful to him, and his whole attention seemed to focus on the particulars, like the arrow in Saint Sebastian's lower abdomen.

He wanted to stay at my place that night because he said he felt haunted. It was like a voice was talking to him at the back of his neck. "No, I'm not going bats," he said. "I'm not hearing voices. I'm just saying it's something *like* that."

He stayed only a couple of hours. He took a shower and filled the place with steam, then sat on the couch in the living room listening to Edith Piaf over and over—the same record, a 45, over and over. He didn't have any underwear and asked to borrow something and another shirt, and maybe socks if I had any. He sat close on the edge of the couch, the shirt on but without any pants and his cock was erect.

Staring at me, he said, "You can look like that painting of Rimbaud. Only you got to put blue mascara around your eyes and draw them upwards like cat's eyes."

Another night, maybe days later, he popped in and said, "You got to wear the bike jacket, man." I figured he wanted me to look like one of the guys in the Third Avenue bar. He said, "Look, we got to try this some kind of way so we can get across the exact feelings, you know what I mean?" I wasn't sure what he meant because it didn't seem to have anything to do with something between us. I wasn't worried about getting into a sexual act with him—it was bisexual and he was the one involving me, coaxing me, as it seemed.

He had a pair of girl's black panties in his jacket pocket and he pulled them out and said, "Hey, these are right off a chick." He hauled them up and sort of stretched them out and plunked them around, and then he tossed them at me.

I could smell perfume.

He said, "Why don't you put them on and then cover over the top part of you, like with something because you don't have tits," and he laughed. He said, "But you can lay there and show me your stomach and see if I get a hard-on."

I said, "Wait a minute, I don't want to do this without drinking something. I mean, who do these underpants belong to?"

He said, "They're just fucking underpants—this chick I know."

130

"Do I know her?" I asked.

He shook his head. "No, just put them on." He got up. "Oh, the light's wrong, man. Where's the candles? Where's the music—that Edith Piaf? You got to pretend you're this French whore—we're in Paris, man. You're this French whore and I'm this guy...."

So we had the lights off and the candle on. I'd yanked out a pint of bourbon, and we passed it back and forth for a few minutes. Gradually I got out of my jeans, just slipping them off slow, like it wasn't what I was really doing. He had the black leather jacket on the bed and I started to put it on.

He said, "No, no, you got to be naked under it—you got to take off your shirt."

Edith Piaf was going, the candle was flickering, and neither one of us had eaten anything. The damn bourbon was burning in my stomach.

He wanted the jacket zipped up, then unzipped a few inches, and then one side closed one way and the other another way. I was barelegged, and with only the black panties on, pulled up high into my crotch and wearing just the black leather jacket.

"Move your leg over this way," he said, "and point your toes, man, like a ballet dancer." Then he said, "Reach into the jacket—the unzipped part—and feel your own tits.... Touch them, and now open the jacket and rub your hand down on your stomach. Put your finger into your belly button and then stick your fingers down into your panties...."

He asked me to keep my hand down in the panties—wanted it sort of flat against myself so my dick didn't show, like I was actually more like a chick. And he wanted me to keep the jacket zipped so he couldn't see them or what I was actually doing in the jacket.

What he did was kiss my legs and jack off, then rolled back on the floor and laughed at the funny scene he'd pretty much orchestrated for what I figured was his own amusement.

He came back later, it might've been the middle of the night, all nervous and rattled. He'd had a fight—"Oh, more than one." he said. After he stayed in the bathtub for an hour playing two sort of musical sticks, he came out with a towel around his waist and sat on the bed. Did I still have those underpants? he asked. I said, yeah—somewhere, but I wasn't in the mood to put them on. We both laughed. He said it would be good if I wanted to suck his cock again, and he started jerking himself off.

"Why don't I get in the bed?" he said, and crawled in beside me. His body was giving off a lot of heat. We fooled around for a few minutes, and then he curled into a ball as if falling asleep, but it sounded like he was sobbing but being quiet about it. I didn't say anything.

About that time he was in rehearsal for the Broadway play, *The Immoralist*. The company was having a terrible time with his "uncommunicative behavior," as they put it. He'd read slow and sullenly, and with little apparent comprehension. What no one seemed to know was that until he'd commit the script to memory, he was unable to formulate what he'd say, so he'd mutter and mumble and make up words, or simply fill space with speech that had nothing to do with the scene.

Rehearsing the play, Louis Jordan complained that "Dean mutters obscenities! He whimpers and grunts and cries and *curses*!" Jimmy only laughed, though he'd told Geraldine Page that until he "experienced the language of the play" in rehearsals, he couldn't get involved, and probably wouldn't until almost the actual opening-night performance. Frustration ran at fever-pitch. Other actors found Jimmy intolerable—impossible to work with. Serious arguments erupted, even to the point of considering whether to fire him. But Geraldine Page rescued him by threatening to walk out if he was dismissed. She insisted he'd be fine by opening night.

The truth was that he'd confided in her and made her swear she'd not repeat what he told her. Geraldine told me a few

Gaeraldine Page and Jimmy backstage during *The Immoralist*. "I saved him from getting fired. They didn't understand him."

years later, "In some peculiar way, Jimmy's difficulties at dealing with the printed page somehow bypassed some other part of him, triggering the most intense concentration of any actor I've worked with. He was like a cat that jumps a great distance without the need to know how far he has to jump."

He attended rehearsals, as a kind of reluctant viewer rather than an actor, wandering around the stage, turning his back to

Geraldine Page, Louis Jordan, Jimmy and Donald Stewart, Going over the play script for *The Immoralist*.

others or mumbling so nobody understood. Louis Jordan said working with "this monster" was the worst experience he'd had in theater.

The play was opening in Philadelphia for its out-of-town tryout when one of Jimmy's ex-roommates wanted to talk to me. He said he was very bothered about the breakup of his friendship with Jimmy. I met him for coffee, but wound up drinking beer. He believed Jimmy was a very lonely individual. "I thought *I* was a maladjusted, miserable, lonely bastard," he said, "but Jimmy takes the cake." He pointed out that Jimmy couldn't be his friend, and he couldn't be my friend. I wasn't sure I understood what he was saying. "He goes through people as fast as he does his underwear," he said, "if he even bothers to put it on half the time." He toasted Jimmy's forthcoming success in the play, saying, "He'll steal the show, you know. I have underestimated my lost friend, James Dean."

He told me that Jimmy's mother had thought up "Byron" for his middle name after the poet Lord Byron, because she somehow "knew" that Jimmy would grow up a cripple or have a crippled soul. It was fitting, he said, since both Byron and Jimmy were cripples.

"Jimmy has said himself," the young man said, "that it's best to be a cripple. Has he told you about his ball-game theory?"

I said no. He summed it up, saying that when one is hurt in the ball game they are called to the sidelines. "From that position, one is offered a vantage point of the whole playing field that can't be appreciated when one is in the game. That way," he said, "the injured one on the sidelines sees more and knows more than those on the field ."

He thought Jimmy was seeking in others the mother he lost as a child. "Though, to these same people," he said, "he can be harmful if not destructive." He said that was the result of another being "impossibly unable" to fill in for Jimmy's dead mother. "No one can," he said, "and in that role he forces upon one, you'll always fail our troubled boy."

Attempting to tell me how much he had been through with Jimmy, he said he was leaving New York in despair, having thrown up his hands. He said, "Once Jimmy has finished with a person, that person ceases to exist. Fini. The end!"

The real reason for our meeting emerged when he asked me if Jimmy and I had been sleeping together. There were 135 rumors. Was that the reason Jimmy was being so hurtful to his friends? "Are you lovers?" he asked, with a kind of weak smile.

At that, I finished our conversation. "You're a sad character, you know?" I said. "You'd be enough to drive anyone to the sidelines."

He raised his glass in a mock toast. "The playing field is yours," he said, "and with all the blessings *and* the curses."

I didn't see Jimmy's ex-pal again in New York.

The play went well in Philadelphia, then successfully opened on Broadway. When the opening-night curtain dropped at eleven o'clock, Jimmy had delivered a masterful, award-winning performance, as well as his three weeks' notice. Everyone was stunned, including his most patient supporter, Geraldine Page. She said, "It was the most unheard-of set of circumstances I'd ever witnessed."

Jimmy told no one of his secret plans to dump the play. Not even Geraldine knew the whole truth, though she had played an unwitting part in the chain of events. A writer she knew, Paul Osborn, was doing a screen adaptation of John Steinbeck's novel *East of Eden* for Elia Kazan and Warner Brothers. Geraldine had talked a great deal about Jimmy's antics, but stressed his peculiar intensity during rehearsals. After Osborn went to the Philadelphia tryouts, he realized Jimmy was the perfect actor for the part of the boyish troublemaker in Steinbeck's story.

Osborn told Kazan, and the director went to take a look at Jimmy. "I got to know him," Kazan said, "and he was an absolutely rotten person. Right away, he was a real cocker and an asshole. But he was the most perfect fucking actor for that part—all bound up in himself with his neurotic problems, lashing out at inappropriate moments; a sulker, an asshole. But absolutely perfect for the role.... There wasn't any question in my mind that he'd bring it off—all he had to do was be himself. The problem I faced was in convincing Warner Brothers that I was going with an unknown, starring him in the movie. I don't know that the big impact

The 'dance' scene from *The Immoralist*.

of this decision really registered with Jimmy—not at that time."

I hadn't seen Jimmy since he'd left for Philadelphia, but I went to the play after it opened at the Royale Theater in New York. He kept talking about plans that were in the works, and he said he couldn't tell anyone why he'd given his notice on opening night. In one scene he did a seductive dance as the homosexual houseboy enticing Louis Jordan. Using a pair of scissors like castanets, Jimmy improvised the snipping sounds as an odd beat to accompany his dance. "It was the strings, man," Jimmy told me, "and Louis Jordan didn't even know what was going on." Jimmy was snipping away at the invisible strings binding Jordan's character to the safer middle-class morality he'd left abroad. In the blaze of the Middle East desert, surrounded with rampant sexuality, Jordan becomes helpless, and Jimmy's snipping with each coaxing step of the dance cut more and more at the man's hopeless respectability. The rigid European gives in, then finally commits suicide.

Jimmy told me his thoughts on the scissors when he called with a vague and muttered story about money being hidden in his apartment. He was going out of town on something important and had to alert me that he might need a favor—someone to go to his apartment and take care of a couple of things—including sending something out of town. I later learned that he'd called Billy Gunn, a girl who worked at Actors' Studio, and Betsy Palmer, with similar stories. It was his way of saying, "See you later," without giving away any secrets. Kazan had warned him not to talk to anyone about the movie until they had completed tests in New York, and until the studio had rubber-stamped the director's decision. With hardly anyone knowing it, Jimmy had fulfilled his prophesy—he'd become the most important actor in town.

Though we'd get together in Hollywood, that was the last time I talked to him on the phone in New York. Soon, with most of his clothes and belongings stuffed into paper sacks, Jimmy was on a plane heading west, "to shake the shit out of Hollywood."

11.

Lost in Paradise

It seemed to many that Jimmy left Broadway quickly—simply vanishing. The few people in the know realized that he was on to something big. At first they thought he'd landed the lead onstage in *Tea and Sympathy*.

Barry Shrode says, "I wasn't sure what had happened to him—people were saying, 'Where's Jimmy, what's he doing?' He'd just finished a Broadway show—had he disappeared? Had he been *kidnapped*?

"A little while later the Studio started getting publicity from the Coast about Jimmy. He was starring in an Elia Kazan movie and touted as the most important movie-star discovery since Brando. It had happened so fast, so unexpectedly. Jimmy was a movie star and nobody'd even seen him in a movie!"

"Kazan," Steve Ross says, "was the magic name. At the time he was considered as a director in the same way that Brando was considered an actor. Kazan was an artistic director—he cared about his work from an artistic point of view, not just the money involved. He was the artist-director of Broadway, and it was a real coup to be in a Kazan film or a Kazan play."

On the airplane to Los Angeles with Jimmy, Kazan recalls him staring out the plane window. "I felt sorry for him. He'd never been in an airplane and he was scared but excited. He didn't know what to expect next. I kept visualizing shots with him—kept seeing how we were going to shoot him from certain angles."

Jimmy's face, which Kazan found "poetic," was actually crooked—a distortion, as if the left eye were pulled downward at the far corner, because it was lower on the face than the right eye. The structure of the skull itself was unusual, leading to a hollowing beneath the high cheekbones and a protrusion of mouth and chin. But it was the "crookedness" of his face that really bothered Dean.

Hollywood sculptor Kenneth Kendall would encounter Dean later that year, aware of the crookedness when he began to sculpt a bust of Jimmy, one requested by Jimmy himself on his visit to Kendall's studio with a one-legged girl. "You'll notice in many pictures that he's got his left cheek resting in his hand. There seems to be this constant reaching up to his own face, as if one side of it was slipping down or collapsing."

Nevertheless, Jimmy's face, according to one of many like-minded cinematographers, "was probably among the most expressive faces in the world. When looking through the camera, I see the way a face is put together differently than it appears in normal life. Usually the more difficult it is to key, the more potential it has for expressiveness."

Arriving in L.A., Kazan says, "Dean had no money to speak of—he had a few dollars and a pocketful of loose change and a knife. He hardly had any clothes with him. He said he didn't have any friends to stay with and we talked about a room or a hotel near the studio temporarily, until something more permanent could be set up while the picture was in production."

Earlier, Jane Deacy had contacted a West Coast agent, Dick Clayton at Famous Artists, about representing Jimmy in Los Angeles. Though Dick Clayton would later claim a friendship with Jimmy dating from before Jimmy went to New York, when they'd worked together in a picture at Universal, the facts do not seem to support Clayton's contentions.

He had told a colleague, "Oh yeah, Jane called me and arranged for me to meet him and I'd have to call Warner Brothers because at the moment there wasn't another number she had for Dean, and she didn't know where he'd even be staying. Somehow he was under the right hand—in a soft glove—of Kazan, who was guarding himself as well, covering his tail in connection with this kid, who Jane loved, but said might be troublesome. This was the golden opportunity of a lifetime, certainly for Jimmy."

No one knew where Jimmy was except Kazan. He seemed to be housed in various offices on the Warners lot while further tests were being made.

Kazan had a plan: He wanted Dick Davalos, who had been cast as Jimmy's brother in *East of Eden*, to get acquainted with Jimmy—tightly, uncomfortably—which they did. "The conflict and tensions between the two would work perfectly for the picture," Kazan said, "plus I knew Davalos would keep an eye on Jimmy. They could be like brothers in real life as well."

Arrangements were made for the two young actors to share a small apartment above a drugstore across the street from Warners in Burbank.

Rudy Berman from Warners would also keep an eye on Jimmy to "keep him posted on the schedule. They were doing tests and ready to go on location, which was up in northern California in Mendocino and the Salinas Valley. We were pressed for time and Kazan wanted Dean to put on a couple of pounds and get some sun—get a little exercise. He had these big bags under his eyes and he looked like he'd stepped out of a New York alley."

Dick Davalos had a more punctual attitude, says Rudy. "He'd be up early doing push-ups and other exercises while Jimmy'd still be in the sack—usually smoking if he was awake. I said, 'Hey! We got to get our asses in gear!' He told me he was a night person. He wasn't used to getting up early.

"Once we were really running late and Jimmy was still in his bed, on his side, facing away from Dick who was dressed and combing his hair. Jimmy was looking at a magazine. I said it was time and Dick jumped into action, but Jimmy stayed in bed and didn't make a move to get up. I said, 'Better go, Jimmy, we can get some chow,' and he turned a page of the magazine. He was doing it defiantly, the little prick, didn't want to be told what to do. Dick didn't mind. I'd tell him, 'Let's go, Dick—let's get it moving.' If I said to Jimmy, 'You want to come along? If you don't want to, you can work it out with the boss'— he'd get himself ready after that because it'd seem like he had a choice, had to do it his way, and he'd follow us at a distance—sort of just like that scene in the movie where he's tagging after Dick and Julie Harris."

"Looking back" Rudy says, "I thought maybe Jimmy didn't like me, and that bothered me but later on he looked me up on one of the sets one morning and he had a wrapped-up package he handed to me. I asked what it was and he said it was a present for me. I said 'What for?' He said, 'It's your birthday—isn't it?' He was right, of course it was my birthday, but I didn't know he knew or gave a damn. I opened the package and it was a beautiful new briefcase. Made out of English leather—had straps and buckles. Really a lovely gift. I said 'For God's sakes, Jimmy, this must've cost you a few bucks. How come you're buying *me* a present?'

"He said, 'Oh, Rudy, I like you, man. I think you're a cool

143

guy. You're not like most of these assholes around here.'"

Jimmy stayed close to Kazan, hooked by the director's devices. "It was like he was attached to Gadge by invisible handcuffs," says Sol Rosen. "One meeting I had with Kazan and Jack Warner and a couple others, Dean was out in the secretary's office on the couch, curled up sleeping with a magazine over his face."

Kazan said he had a live wire on his hands. Laughing, he said he wasn't talking about a dangerous character, but that Jimmy was an "undisciplined person" who could be disciplined into the most brilliant efforts with the right handling—with the right attention. "What you see," he said, "is what you're getting."

At first Jimmy was without a car, without a place to sleep. Before the apartment with Davalos, he'd been in a motel for a couple of days or staying with a relative "way out the other side of West Los Angeles." Too far away, Kazan said. He couldn't have Dean running around loose.

"We met in the office," Sol rememebreds. "Kazan stood there looking down at the kid for a few moments, and pointed down to a hole in one of Dean's soles. Kazan rumpled him awake and Dean sat up. He said, 'Yeah. Okay, what's up?' Kazan introduced us and said, 'Sol's going to take care of some details with you and get things fixed up for you, like a place to stay. We're going to put you up across the street. It's a grand idea since you don't have a car.'"

Jimmy said, "Across the street from right here?"

"Yeah," Kazan said. "It's right across the street, and you got the little drugstore downstairs to get coffee and everything else will be taken care of."

"You mean my meals and eating and that stuff?" Jimmy asked.

"Right," Kazan said. "You go with Sol and he's taking you to over to publicity to get photos and biography and then we'll be all set to go."

Kazan, Brando, Julie Harris and Jimmy. Kazan brought Brando to the Eden set "hoping he'd give Jimmy a kick in the ass."

One of the tests Jimmy had made was with Paul Newman, earlier considered for the same part. Though symmetrically almost perfect compared to Jimmy's, Newman's face seemed unable to produce more than a few set and determined expressions. Jimmy's face, on the other hand, photographed as though each pocket and mound of its features had a separate life—the same thing he'd once said about Tallulah Bankhead. His nervous tension especially flushed and rippled through his features, forming expressions that never seemed to duplicate themselves. From every angle, the face took on a different look.

From the beginning, Kazan was convinced that he had the actor he needed. He later said, "I chose Jimmy because he was Cal, the younger brother. There was no point in casting further. Jimmy was it. He had a grudge against all fathers. He was vengeful. He had a sense of aloneness and of being persecuted. He was suspicious. He could make himself hateful and he was absolutely perfect for the picture."

Kazan realized that it was only a matter of convincing Warner Brothers to shoot without a star. Since even Kazan admits that he could do no wrong with the Warner Brothers people at the time, it was not long before they began to bend to his wishes.

When comparing *East of Eden* to his previous films, Kazan said, "[It] is more personal to me. It is my own story. One hates one's father, one rebels against him. Finally one cares for him, one recovers oneself, one understands him, one forgives him. You're no longer afraid of him, you have accepted him."

But at that point in Jimmy's life there could be no forgiveness, there could be no acceptance of a figure that, as he put it, "is supposed to be greater than me... supposed to have this power at his command to make the children dance." Jimmy saw Winton rarely; the talk was strained, the pleasantness forced. There was nothing to say. The visits stopped.

The grudges against his father, so embedded in Jimmy, were overwhelmingly brought into focus in *East of Eden*, and millions would respond to its impact. It reached suddenly, and directly, into their most basic emotions. Kazan knew this—it was what he was working towards—"something that comes along so damned rare," he said. "I believed this picture could have the power to reach directly into the psychological heart of the viewer."

Perhaps, too, it manipulated the audience in the same way that Kazan manipulated Dean, stirring in many that sense of rebellion against the father. "Getting even with him," was what Jimmy said about the role he played.

A film actor's life can be measured largely by the movies he's made. One meets the project, commits oneself to it, engages in it—marries it, and consummates the sometimes passionate love affair.

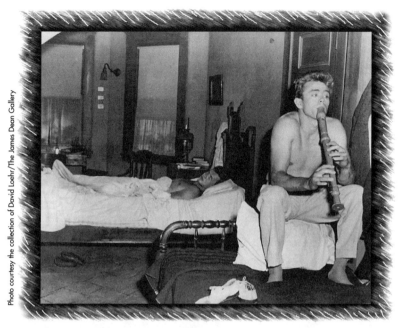

Scene with Dick Pavalos cut from East of Eden; due to studios fear of possible "sexual implications."

There was no young, serious actor at that time who wouldn't have sold his soul to Satan to star in an Elia Kazan film. It was as simple at that. A Kazan film was the pinnacle. There'd be no turning back. Obscurity was gone. You'd arrived as an actor in the best, most important manner.

No one knew this more than Jimmy—a Brando nut; worshipping at Kazan's altar of artfulness, integrity, and importance.

And of course, it was the screen adaptation of a notable novel by a prestigious American writer, although John Steinbeck didn't personally like James Dean.

Not too many did.

Julie Harris, his costar, the eternal mother-sister, adored him as an exotic, rare find.

Julie Harris, like Geraldine Page, dicovered a closeness with Jimmy she found hard to share with others.

The making of *East of Eden* was a unique Hollywood experience. On screen perfection was created that could never be duplicated. To use his own term, it was the synchronization of all Jimmy had learned, all he knew, all that New York and Hollywood had brought, into one package. It was exactly what he'd talked about with Eartha. All the chemistry came together—even Lenny Rosenman composing the score.

"What's happened," Jimmy told Eartha, "can never happen again. It's perfect and you can't make improvements on what's perfect. You can't square a square any more than it's square."

Jimmy held loosely, almost obligingly, to those friends he'd left in New York. Feeling alone and adrift, he kept a string looped around Barbara by a series of letters he wrote to her bemoaning his loneliness and his isolation, and his "California virginity." It was also like an anchor line to New York and his apartment on Sixty-third Street. With that anchor line still attached, he was free *not* to be who he thought he should've been in New York.

He was now somebody else. The new, upcoming movie star had to be promoted accordingly. Warner's publicity department told him, "It's kind of like being a prince. One night you go to bed and you think it's just going to be another day, but the next morning you find you're a prince. It's a great responsibility—being a prince. You have to live and act like a prince."

Jimmy wouldn't listen to them. He said, "I wake up the same person every morning. I'm an actor and I came out here to act. I didn't come out here to be a prince or a social fop or a gilded dandelion."

Sol Rosen says, "I remember walking with Jimmy behind the front buildings one of the days right after they'd come back from Salinas and he was dragging his heels, hands stuffed in his pockets and scowling at everyone he'd pass. He'd asked where we were going, and I said to get things squared away with the department and he said he was hungry—they hadn't fed him. I said, 'You want to get something to eat first? Okay.' We went to the commissary and then I saw his face brighten up the first time that day.

"We'd gotten our lunch and he said, 'Sheez, there's Jack Palance. Who's that girl with him? What movie is she making?'

"'Who?' I asked. He was pointing with his fork to Pier Angeli. I told him they were in *The Silver Chalice*. Jimmy said, 'Oh, that's that fucking religious story.' I said that was more or less what it was. He said, 'Well, tell me about her.' I said a few things I knew and he nodded nonchalantly. 'She's a pretty girl,' and he said he'd like to meet her.

"Right then the thought hit me—a bug of an idea, and I said, 'You want to meet Pier?'

"He said, 'Naw—I don't know. Well, sure, why not? She's got an Italian princess face, doesn't she? Sure, let's meet her.'

"After a few minutes I said hello to Palance and we talked for a second and then I introduced Jimmy to Palance and to Pier. Jimmy just nodded and said, 'How're you doing?'

"She said, 'I'm doing fine. How are you doing?'

"He said he was doing fine.

"'How do you like working with Mr. Kazan?'

"He shrugged. 'He's okay. He's great. We got together in New York.'

"I said Jimmy was from New York. He'd been on Broadway when arrangements were made for the picture.

"Pier said she'd heard quite a bit about it. She asked him how he liked living in Los Angeles now, and he said he didn't like it so much. 'I'm spending too much time out here. I want to get back to New York pretty soon.' He sort of shrugged and gave her a distant look, squinting at her. 'You're Italian— from Italy?' he asked.

"'Yes, I am,' she said, and then I could see that they'd pretty much exhausted the conversation and we said good-bye.

"He sort of watched after her and said, 'She's pretty but she's stuck-up. Everyone out here's so fucking stuck up it's enough to make you sick to your stomach.' He imitated someone throwing up—gagging—and a few people looked at him.

"'That's James Dean,' one of them said.

"I laughed, patting him, joking a little because I was frankly embarrassed. He could be truly embarrassing. Some people said he was so shy—so soft-spoken and withdrawn— but whenever I saw something like that I knew it wasn't so much withdrawn and shy as kind of surly and noncommunicative. Maybe he was shy with some other people.

"Working on this idea, I asked him how he'd like to go out

on a date with Pier, like to a movie premiere? Kazan had a closed set and Jimmy wasn't talking to any outside press—no publicity except what might come out of Warner's.

"He said, 'I don't know about a premiere, man.'

"They could get to know one another a little better, I suggested, and maybe he wouldn't think she was so stuck-up. 'She's actualy quite a charming young lady,' I told him. Maybe it could be arranged.

"He said okay."

Rosen met with Ted Ashton, who had been assigned to handle publicity for the movie. They talked a little about the idea of Dean and Pier Angeli being seen around and starting up some sparks that the reporters and columnists might pick up, even with Kazan's gag restrictions.

"I said Jimmy liked the girl, seemed interested, and maybe we could get a few shots of them together. Jack Warner thought it was a good idea," says Rosen. "Two pictures—*Eden* and *Silver Chalice*—could benefit well. With Ashton wondering where it could lead, I got a green light on a little extracurricular work.

"It is amazing how [the press] run when they get a hot piece in the air. Later I'd see the scene as a lot of dogs when you throw a soup bone in their midst. They make up stories, they pad their items. They try to scoop each other—cut each other's throats, and I think Jimmy got to believe some of the stories himself."

Jimmy was totally "press stupid," as Rosen put it. To these studio people, he appeared as an introverted oddball in their midst, there because of an amazing gift—that of being an exceptional actor.

"A lot of rich ground," Rosen says, "rich areas to plumb like the new Marlon Brando image, booting Marlon off the throne." Jimmy might not have seemed cooperative, but he wasn't going to disappoint them.

"I don't think he basically liked any of us, or trusted anyone associated with the press. He smelled your motive a mile away, and only if he felt it would serve his purposes, he'd let you have the ounce of fat for what he felt might be a pound of meat coming back his way."

12.

Loose Maverick

66 **J**immy's fucking Pier Angeli in the dressing room," Kazan said. "I hear them through the walls, either grunting and groaning or fighting like a couple of characters out of a comic book."

Rosen managed to gather a "wad" of material on the two stars and had "shot it out" to the media. "We kicked the ball off with Hedda Hopper and Skolsky, and Pier and Jimmy were running around a little, getting their pictures taken. "Only, he came in after a couple weeks and said he wanted us to cancel—he used the word cancel—this romance bullshit between Pier and myself.'

"I went through a long-winded explanation of why we were busting our balls to get the press to look favorably upon him, and certainly favorably upon a healthy, positive relationship that he *pretended* to cultivate with Pier Angeli, explaining that this might get a smile out of Sheilah Graham instead of a knife in our ribs.

"Jimmy looked at me and said, 'Fuck Sheilah Graham. The only good thing about Sheilah Graham is she used to be fucking Scott Fitzgerald.' He stared at me as cold as ice and gave me a speech I'd heard from him already maybe six times. 'I don't play this fucking game,' he said. 'You can't make me play this fucking game. It's *your* act, man, and I don't want any part of it. I am here to be an actor—not a goddamn social butterfly…. I'm an *actor*—I'm *serious* about what I'm doing…. I don't live in this goddamn zoo,' he said, 'I live in *New York*!'"

The same speech, as Rosen said, they'd all been hearing from Dean. His agent at Famous Artists—Dick Clayton— kept saying, Don't pay any attention to him. He might bitch but he'll go out and do it.

"Dean went off on a tangent and then he got up and walked out—leaving me without any more sense to it as when we'd sat down. My recommendation to the front office was go ahead and do it and it wasn't necessary to have his cooperation or involvement in it.

"I was learning that he'd never kick that we were doing it, and frankly I thought he loved it—one of these hard-asses, but it's not the only side to the coin. He wasn't a Greta Garbo—she genuinely *was* opposed to publicity. Not Jimmy. The son of a bitch loved it. You could see him grinning all over but trying to show he didn't give a damn. He loved it but didn't want you to think he did. I actually thought he was afraid to commit himself—afraid to get on his own bandwagon—for whatever reason, I don't know. That was between him and his God, or his shrink."

According to Rosen, Pier, on the other hand, was a "publicity-crazed gal" who didn't care what something said as long as she saw herself in print. She devoured herself in print like a fat lady swallowing chocolate drops.

Viewing Warners, and other studios' publicity departments

as "artists in a bell jar," Rosen said they operated in an enclosed space "logistically separate from the rest of the world."

At one time, not so long ago, the only unforgivable sin in the hermetically sealed world of Hollywood was to air dirty laundry at large beyond the "impenetrable dome," or to lie and let them catch you lying. By so doing, said Rosen, "you become an unforgivable renegade, an outcast who'll never work again in this town."

The press and the trades had carte blanche in the department of make-believe. "This is because what *they* say, the public wants to hear. The millions of fans need a certain fodder fit for their appetites. They cannot digest anything else."

Kazan had moved Jimmy from the Olive Drugstore apartment onto the soundstage and into a dressing room next to his own. "I'm going to have to keep a hold on him at all times," Kazan told his production manager, "never let him out of my sight."

The director believed he'd brought out to the surface, the raw guts of experience in Dean, and he wanted to shape it as he went—knowing that with the fury and explosiveness he'd brought forth and onto the screen, there'd be "a backlash" with Jimmy. He'd get difficult—maybe even a little nuts— "not that he already wasn't," Kazan said. "He had violence in him, he had a hunger within him, and he was himself the boy that he played in the film."

As he did with many others, Jimmy managed to put Kazan on edge at moments. The director would become irritated with him, bothered by wanting to reshape him. He called Dean a "cocker" and thought he was "sick, twisted," and generally headed for trouble. He felt that the violent scenes in the movie were extensions of Dean's basic problems, "things he just came upon of his own."

Jimmy was not like Brando. Kazan felt there was little

similarity between the two; Brando was a multitalented person, a sort of stream of experience that could be tapped, then directed to flow as openly as if the actor were stripping himself psychologically and laying out, naked and vulnerable for the world, the many facets of human personality.

But Jimmy had very little pliability, according to the director. His vulnerability appeared hidden behind "one hurt, a one sort of hurt" that Jimmy played upon again and again. It came on so strong that audiences felt an immediate need to protect and shelter him. And yet underneath the small child—seen so clearly in those bean fields in the movie, the way Kazan plays the smallness of Dean against the vast fields—there was the violence, a muted aggression that could give way at any moment to destructiveness.

It was summer as the company was finishing the movie, and Jimmy was extremely sensitive to criticism of his first starring role. Forgetting Kazan, he was openly striving for the kind of fame Brando held as "Hollywood's number one bad boy" some years earlier. Jimmy wanted people around him who would take him on those terms of ambition and fame, and he refused to play the game any other way.

Doubts, fears, and anxieties plagued him through the filming of *East of Eden*—he'd felt cut off, a kind of captive of Kazan's, yet praying for the movie to never be finished. It was as though he'd come to life—truly found his place. He wanted this life to continue, to never end. He'd sink into depressions that bordered on notions of suicide, writing hasty letters to the few in New York he felt he could trust, trying to convey to them the desperation he felt.

They didn't understand.

Though they were "inseparable" for a while, Jimmy's friendship with composer Leonard Rosenman—writing the music for *East of Eden*—broke up quickly in Hollywood.

"We'd come out together from New York and Jimmy was

quite responsible for my landing the work in the picture but a person can only take so much. We went our separate ways for probably a number of reasons, but mainly because the role Jimmy expected me to play in his life—I simply couldn't play…. It was that of a father, and it was exemplified by a fantastic exchange we once had. He was trying to get me to come out and play basketball and I said, 'Well, Jimmy, I don't like sports very much, especially those kinds of sports,' and he kept pressing and pressing and finally I said, 'Why's it so important for you that I go out and play basketball?' And he looked at me and he said, 'Well, you know how a person feels, it's like you want your father to play ball with you.'

"So I blew up. I said, 'I'm not your father, your father's alive and living in Burbank or wherever,' and I said, 'Why don't you call your father and go ask him to play basketball with you?'"

But there was more to it than that. As with others, Rosenman backed away from what he perceived as a kind of "willful, reckless crazing for violence—for the morbid side of life. He seemed to be choosing to see only pain and destruction."

Jimmy's fascination with the spilled blood of matadors had secretly escalated during his short stint in Hollywood. With opportunities for fame abounding, a part of him tried desperately to undermine his success.

Though *East of Eden*, especially Jimmy's performance, would soon be highly praised by many critics, his vengeance disturbed those reviewers writing for upper-middle-class women readers whose sensibilities they must titillate but not offend—reviewers such as Sloan Wilson, Herman Wouk, and John O'Hara, who wrote in *Collier's* that Kazan had Dean "squirm and twist in a way that reminded me of Fanny Brice as Baby Snooks doing the old revue routine of reciting while wanting to go to the bathroom." O'Hara was critical, too, of Kazan's use of horse shit in the street scenes. And when Dean was not fighting off an urgency to go to the bathroom, wrote O'Hara, "he is skipping and dashing about like a village idiot."

Six years later in 1961, *East of Eden* was reissued in Europe. The London *Sunday Times* reviewer wrote, "When *East of Eden* first appeared, it was fashionable to say that Dean tried to imitate Brando. Well, if he tried he certainly didn't succeed, and in the result the only resemblance I can see is in the use of the broken, half-masticated phrase.

"Brando is all power: power sometimes pinioned, or trapped, or degraded, but still power. James Dean was sentenced by physique to stand for defenselessness; and some instinct, far more than the actor's technique, taught him how to suggest, behind the mask of rebelliousness, a different being, shrinking, fragile, not quite fully grown. As long as he stuck to that he had no equal; and looking again at this first film I am astounded by his performance. It is even better than I had thought: more truly anguished, more delicately poised between the awkward, sulky scapegoat and the young creature exploding with love. It gives heart and center to the film, it breathes life into Kazan's melodramatics. Perhaps as an actor James Dean was lucky to die half-tried, before he could be forced out of his adolescent's shell. In *East of Eden*, at any rate, his wistful image is undisturbed."

"The more success an actor has," Kazan said in an interview with *Cahiers du cinéma*, "the more he acquires the look of wax fruit—he is no longer devoured by life. I try to catch my actors at the moment when they are still human. If you have a human actor, you can slip yourself inside, touch him and wake him."

Yet it appeared to Kazan that neither he nor anyone else could twist Jimmy free of the emotions surrounding his bitter childhood. Jimmy seemed to cling to these guarded memories as one might perpetually clutch in his palm a child's jack with sharpened points.

About Pier Angeli, Jimmy said, "I had the feeling I was being smothered by her—not by her physically, I mean, but by something else—some sort of clinging, enveloping thing that kept pushing up against me. I was being crowded to do something I didn't want to do."

Much later, Pier said she had felt overly controlled as a child; her mother was zealously Catholic and Pier felt that she had developed an outwardly unseen, but somewhat "morbid streak," she called it, which had caught Jimmy's attention immediately.

"He seemed to see something in me that I didn't want to look at and wasn't willing to include as part of myself. Not that he was in control of what he saw. He smelled it out in a person, brought it out, perhaps. It was dark and gloomy. There was a kind of danger to it that caused me to feel threatened. You could say I felt unsafe.... Not that Jimmy could ever deliberately have done anything to put harm in my way. It was more of a combination of extreme sensibilities."

The kind of "delightful romance" the fans had been so gullibly chasing, conjured by the Warners Brothers studio publicity, had nothing to do with reality. So little was ever shown of Pier's "gloomy side" that any revelation might've seemed a shock except to those exposed to her mental turmoils, later complicated by her addiction to drugs.

Something churning in the lovely young woman with the dark eyes latched on to Jimmy like a organism, something so wildly sexual and chaotic in her nature that she sought punishment for her defiance of those early Catholic bonds. This would eventually push Pier to suicide. The trouble was lurking long before Hollywood and her "discovery" by screenwriter Stewart Stern, brought in from New York to write the script for *Rebel Without a Cause*, Jimmy's next picture.

While finishing *Eden*, Jimmy's infrequent "pileups" with Pier resembled "a hopeless emotional grappling for something that wasn't there." The scenes continued in the dressing room Jimmy now called home. He said, "She'd corner me with her dumb preoccupations because we'd fucked, and I thought I'd chase her away with what she said was *my* 'volcano of need,' but I'll tell you this: Miss Pizza's the one you can call a volcano—but there's no hot lava shooting out of her."

The side of the coin that the fan magazines knew nothing about was a rapid cooling of the friendship, at least on Jimmy's part, while Pier snatched at other involvements, other relationships, never letting on to her new lovers that she'd been intimate with Jimmy.

He had his own problems. He made it clear he didn't need Pier's.

When *Eden* was finished, Jimmy stayed in his dressing room. He didn't want to leave the set, and remained holed up on the soundstage, hiding from studio security officers. He ate tuna from cans and packages of potato chips, and tried to read magazines by the dim glow of the Zippo cigarette lighter given to him by the actor Albert Dekker.

Alone on the soundstage one night, Julie Harris heard "sobbing and moaning sounds coming from somewhere in the darkened stage." She traced the noise to the dressing room that had been occupied by Jimmy. "He was still *there!*" Julie says.

She found him on the bare floor of the dressing room, crying and moaning. "I held him in my arms," Julie says, "and I thought, Good lord, this is a continuation of the picture! He didn't want it to be over.

"He felt completely rejected because we'd finished the picture and it was time for everybody to come home. He felt very, very alone because it was all over. He said it was as if someone had died—had left him alone. Everyone usually becomes very close during filming.

"You become a family, and when it's finished it can be quite sad at times, because you've made so many wonderful friends, and though you've sworn you're going to keep on being friends, you know in your heart that it isn't so. But I have never seen someone so completely devastated by the inevitable—by the end of that kind of social world that's developed during the long months of shooting a picture.

"I said, 'You have to go home, Jimmy,' and he said he didn't have a home. He was living in that dressing room anyway, and he was being kicked out. I thought he was having a nervous breakdown."

Jimmy was ordered by the studio to "relocate" himself off the lot. "No one can live on a soundstage," he was told. "It's not only against fire regulations, it's downright *crazy*."

But Jimmy *was* crazy, Kazan says. Not like someone who runs around in a Napoleon hat or the wayward brother you have to keep locked in the back room, "though that was worth considering," the director said. "He was twisted inside.... He was sick. He was actually a very disturbed young man—sick. He was in bad need of some help—some psychological help. From what I understand, he never got it."

Agent Dick Clayton came up with a small apartment north of Sunset Boulevard on Sunset Plaza Drive—the same area where Jimmy'd shared time with Rogers Brackett, now an unmentioned name vanishing in the exhaust smoke of Jimmy's past.

"You can get a rotten complex about not making it as an actor," Jimmy once said about Dick Clayton. "He's a great guy, an excellent agent, but he wanted to make it as an actor more than ever thinking about being an agent." Jimmy went on to say that Dick was somehow experiencing an actor's success "by proxy," he said, through handling Jimmy's business affairs.

Dick was neither effeminate nor faggoty, except maybe after he'd loosened up with a few drinks—kicked off his pants and danced around, as he once did at his small homestead cabin in Palm Desert, falling back on the mattress to throw apart his legs and wave them in the air like an old whore.

In Hollywood, Dick occupied a single apartment in a one-story, "Hawaiian-like" complex on Norton Avenue off Sweetzer, a block north of Santa Monica Boulevard. He slept on a pull-down Murphy bed and kept a portrait of himself in a white sailor suit nearby.

When I first met Dick through Jimmy, the agent was actively working on Tab Hunter's career—having fallen in step with Henry Willson. Jimmy said, "Dick's the best around because he takes a personal interest—he can be a pal and a friend and cares about what you do."

Dick Clayton was my agent for a while and we spent time in Palm Desert with Tab Hunter and another boy who slept on a fold-down couch and mattress on the floor.

The cabin consisted of one large room on the land Dick had homesteaded through the Los Angeles County Land Office in City Hall. It was a short walk through the desert to the Shadow Mountain Country Club, adjacent to Palm Springs.

I spent a couple weekends in the desert with Dick and Tab, watching Tab dive from the high boards at the country-club pool. Jimmy sometimes drove out to Palm Desert—more for the fast drive from L.A. on the Palm Springs road than to hang around "Dick's shack" for a day or so. Once he took a blonde, an up-and-coming young foreign actress, to Dick's for a Saturday spin in his new sports car, a Porsche Speedster. He said they'd didn't stay overnight because "she didn't have anything to talk about," but gave him "a good blowjob" because his cock could "go all the way into her empty head."

Later, Dick negotiated the loan-out deal with Warners for Jimmy to costar in *Somebody Up There Likes Me*, with Pier

Angeli at MGM. The deal was intended to give Warners the chance to milk the "romance" between Jimmy and Pier that had been pathetically stretched through publicity for more than three months. "We'd had saturation bombing," says Rosen. "And any linking of the two, romance-wise, short of marriage— especially with them romancing in the picture— meant big box office clout for everybody."

Apart from Kazan, few others anticipated Jimmy's volatile mood swings or the depth of his personal confusions being kindled by his sudden success. Pier told me later, in characteristically dramatic fashion, "I brought out in Jimmy the small boy that he kept locked in his heart—or in his mind. This small boy was a very troubled one. He wanted me to love him unconditionally, but Jimmy was not able to love someone else in return, that is with any deep feeling for that other person. He wanted to be loved. It was the troubled boy that wanted to be loved very badly. I loved Jimmy as I have loved no one else in my life, but I could not give him the enormous amount that he needed. It emptied me. Loving Jimmy was something that could empty a person. There was no other way to be with Jimmy except to love him and be emptied of yourself."

Jimmy never had it in mind to marry Pier. He faked it. To people whom he thought the idea would please, he suggested the "possibility of matrimony" with a sly grin, but on the practical side, he was more concerned about the horse he'd bought and what it ate—he never gave a hoot about "wedding bells." He said, "She's screwing half the city, so let her marry one of those jokers."

Which she did. Quickly. To her previous, Italian Catholic boyfriend—singer Vic Damone.

A few reporters asked Jimmy if he was upset, and for these hounds, he put on the hanging-head attitude. It was amusing to watch Jimmy sap sympathy from those he wanted to feel

Shooting a roll of Pier Angeli during the studio's "romance" build-up between the two.

sorry for him. One reporter concocted the story that Jimmy rode his motorcycle to the church where Pier was marrying Damone, and that he sat across the street gunning the engine.

In reality, describing himself as an "existential pencil" which composed the final act long before it occurred, Jimmy confessed no sense of loss. He would, however, act out the "poor soul" injured to the hilt for those who'd understand the "conventional approach," and readily applaud Jimmy's performance of *"Woe is me, oh, woe is me!"*

Behind his hand, he said, "Fuck them both—who the fuck needs them?" It wasn't much different, he said, than throwing a horny hog into a hot pen with a saucy sow. "You find people who nobody needs," he said, "and in a flash they find each other."

13.

Rebel Without Remorse

I'd been out of New York for months. I'd done a play in the Bay Area, and was back in Hollywood making a screen test for a possible contract with Paramount Pictures. It was early spring of 1955, and I hadn't seen Jimmy in a while. One day I pulled into Googie's parking lot on my bike, this one a BSA, and saw him sitting on the seat of his own bike, a Triumph. He was wearing an expensive black leather British bike jacket with a fur collar, and tan cowhide gloves. A photographer was taking pictures of him posing with his bike.

Jimmy had clip-on sunglasses over his regular glasses and stared at me as I stopped in a space near his bike. He gave a little salute and said, "Hey, *atado*, what's happening, man?" Cool and distant, untrusting maybe. That would soon disappear during our first few talks.

What caught me off-guard was that he was running around with an odd bird I'd known around town for a few years—Jack Simmons. He had the reputation of being "one of the most

After Kazan brought him to Hollywoood, Jimmy said he was "a freak..." and "an alien from outer space..."

notorious faggots" in Hollywood. Jimmy would later ask me about Jack, and I told him how we met—in front of the Tropical Village, a gay bar on the boardwalk at Santa Monica. Jack had long dark hair and a big hook nose in those days.

They called him "the Hawk," and when I met him he was wearing pink bathing trunks, cut high on the sides with some sort of Indian beaded belt. He had on a pair of white sunglasses and was trying to dance with different guys. The bar was usually jammed on the weekends, and it wouldn't have been unusual to spot Rock Hudson or Dan Dailey dancing somewhere deep in the place.

Someone I'd worked on a show with invited me in for a sandwich, and Jack stopped me on the boardwalk. He said he recognized me and wanted to buy me a drink. I said it wasn't a good idea because I wasn't even seventeen yet, and the whole place might've gotten into a jam. He insisted on a Dr. Pepper, and we talked outside the bar. After that, he was chasing me, calling at night, driving me places I'd have to be, but never seriously tried to put the make on me.

Now he'd had his nose bobbed and combed his hair like Jimmy, who'd landed him a small part in *Rebel*. While the "new star" halo was shining over Jimmy, it was people like Jack—as well as myself—that puzzled Hollywood. A reject, dubbed a pitiful fringe-nut in Hollywood's substratum, Jack had captured Jimmy's interest with an unwavering, doglike devotion.

In times to come, Jack would be described as being an "unknown" screwball who'd somehow attached himself to Jimmy after the release of *East of Eden*. Actually, when *Life* magazine's huge spread on Jimmy ran the previous March, Jack made up his mind to meet Jimmy and become his closest friend. Begging and badgering his way through others he knew, Jack managed to infiltrate the Warners' lot. He succeeded in cornering his newfound idol, and began a campaign of laying himself down as Jimmy's personal doormat.

.... "What's '*atado*'?" Jack asked me after that first day in Googie's parking lot. "Why's Jimmy calling you that? What's '*atado*' mean?" Later he said, "It's got to do with a fucking bull—a fucking animal—tying it up or using a rope so it means some kind of state of *peace*—what bullshit! What kind of peace are you offering Jimmy?"

I didn't say anything.

Rarely quoted and known by very few, Jack Simmons was destined to become one of the most mysterious characters in Jimmy's history, with most of the tidbits about him coming from another mutual friend, Maila Nurmi, the would-be actress and self-professed "witch" then calling herself Vampira. Dressing in black like Morticia of the Addams Family, Maila hosted a television show of old spooky movies—the forerunner of late-night TV horror gimmicks.

While Jack was reticent—almost never talking about Jimmy to others—Vampira freely concocted stories about Jimmy, crediting herself via movie magazines and other publications as being his "lover." She created publicity for herself, for her television show, and unwanted notoriety for Jack, chauffeuring Maila around in an old black hearse.

It was through Jack's possessive attachment to Jimmy that Maila was ushered into briefly become part of the "night watch," as we were called—or, by some columnists, a "crew of creeps." Already columns had started mentioning the handful of characters Dean had collected who made up the "night watch," one noting that "what gaucheries Dean doesn't think up, these sycophants do."

The all-night jams in Googie's, the bikes and stunts, were mostly construed by reporters as crazy antics to shock and deride the accepted Hollywood system. Jimmy apparently reveled in the sour publicity. He was creating a language of physical and psychological impact, a dangerous image that radiated from the screen and tabloid papers. The stories kept repeating hints of danger—of impending disaster that would somehow visit itself on the hot new screen star—proving himself to be a disagreeable oddball. Jimmy loved it, especially the mentions about "death wishes."

169

In Googie's back booth, Jimmy, Jack Simmons, and a girl named Connie.

Enhancing the public's curiosity were Vampira's innuendos to the press about the "dark romance" between herself and Jimmy, which he'd chuckle over. But most of all, it was the "morbid" appearance of his "crew"—which included myself—that kept the bad publicity cooking. No one knew where it would lead, or what Jimmy intended to do with these "jackals" he'd gathered around himself.

Jimmy's penchant for secrecy kept Jack initially ignorant of the relationship Jimmy and I had shared in New York. At the same time, Jimmy showed no more than a passing curiosity over the fact that Jack and I had been friendly two years before. He did ask, "Did you and Jack get anything going?" I said no, absolutely not. Jimmy said, "He's a very nervous guy…." and laughed.

Like myself, Jack wasn't one of those "fat numb people" who criticized Jimmy, but was quickly a member, as one columnist put it, "of the malcontent rebels" Jimmy surrounded himself with; "frequenting Sunset Boulevard's night hangouts, recklessly racing cars and motorcycles." It was a short-lived moment to be long-remembered by Hollywood.

Jack would later claim that he was in love with Jimmy—the only love of his life, he'd say. Even decades later he'd break down and sob over Jimmy's death. It was as though Jack

Schwab's Pharmacy and Googie's on Sunset Boulevard, the favorite hangouts of Jimmy and "The Night Watch."

would not only lose his "one true love," but his "soul as well." Jack would try to sanitize his relationship with Jimmy, saying, as he did to writer Val Holley: "I never touched Jimmy's organs"— by which, of course, he meant Jimmy's cock.

One night in Googie's, Jimmy said that the line he wanted on his tombstone was from the poet Alan Seeger's diary—"one crowded hour of glorious life" being "worth an age without a name." A telegram was quickly sent to Jack Warner, suggesting an engraved headstone.

The front office didn't appreciate the prank, and promptly clamped down on Jimmy's motorcycle-racing around the studio lot. They began to keep tabs on "the oddballs" Jimmy was palling with. These "tabs," actually file cards, soon became a

Los Angeles 1954. Maila "Vampira" Nurmi. She was after Jimmy's "soul" but didn't even get a kiss.

sort of blackball list of potentially troublesome people—those that might cost the studio unnecessary expenses (following Dean's death, the word "unnecessary" would be changed to "grievous").

The night the telegram was sent, I ran into the actress Irish

McCalla in Googie's. (Irish was starring in a popular television show, *Sheena, Queen of the Jungle*, which was filmed on location in Mexico). She was in a front booth with a couple of people while Jimmy and the crew were in the usual rear booth. We were heading out when Irish looked up at me and then at Jimmy, and I said, "Hey, this is Irish McCalla, who's Sheena, Queen of the Jungle." Jimmy took her hand as if to shake it, but brought her up out of the booth.

She was taller than him and he started to giggle. She was still holding his hand as he mumbled something to her, bowing a little in mock acknowledgment of her royalty as Queen of the Jungle. Then Jimmy said, "I'm gonna come swing in your tree, Sheena." She said that would be all right with her, as she had a lot of slack in the vines. I remember her looking at me and grinning.

When Jimmy asked your opinion, or how something might be "handled from a different perspective," as he'd put it, he was really seeking approval for something he'd already figured out. If you were critical or showed that you were no longer at ease with his antics, then you would be cast into the chorus of what he called "inconsequential grownups" and would no longer be of service to him.

People like Eartha Kitt, now back in L.A., and others whose particular intelligence or talents he valued, were allowed to be critical of his behavior, but they could never be members of the "night watch." We were, as one writer put it "the small handful of sloppily-clad screwballs, quite isolated from the mainstream, whose necessity to Jimmy so disturbs the front office that these hangers-on encouraging his bad-boy behavior are being noted in a way that assures what is called 'blackballing' in Hollywood."

About this time while the filming of *Rebel Without a Cause* was well under way, Jimmy met Karen Davis on the

Warner Brothers lot. She was on the *Rebel* set as an extra when Jimmy grinned at her. He said her sweater looked like a furry skin "about to fly" away from her.

She told him she had an uncle who'd given her a shirt made out of deerskin but it was too big for her, even though he'd suggested she wash it in hot water and let it shrink up.

"We joked around a little," Karen said, "and he said he didn't think deerskin shrank up too good. He said, 'People-skin shrinks,' and then he said maybe the deerskin shirt would fit him.

"I told him I'd bring it to him if I was working the next day, but I didn't think I was, at least I hadn't heard that I was.

"He asked how did I know about it, and I said I had to call in, and keep calling in.

"He said, 'You want to work tomorrow?'

"I said sure—I'd like to bring him the shirt—if I could find it. I said, 'Maybe it's all moldy or something.'

"He thought that was funny and laughed, and then he said, 'If you want to work tomorrow, you tell me now and I'll make sure you do.'

"I said okay—I'd like to work. He said, 'You're as good as working.'

"The deerskin shirt was a mess—falling apart—and I was too embarrassed to bring it with me. When I caught sight of him he looked the other way. He didn't meet my glance for most of the time we were up there, and then on a lunch break this kid came over—it was Jack Simmons—and said, 'Are you Karen?' I said yes. He said, 'Jimmy Dean wants to see you. He said to tell you to come over to the trailer. They're doing make-up right now.'

"I went over and he was sitting in the chair and then he said, 'Where's my shirt?' I told him about it and that I'd been too embarrassed to bring it with me, and then for some reason that made me cry and I wanted to get away from him. He got up—he had some sort of cardboard thing around his neck to keep the makeup from his shirt, and he put his arm on me and said, 'You want to go for a ride on a motorcycle? You ever ridden on a bike?'

"I said when I was little—the same uncle who'd made the shirt had taken me for a ride on a big motorcycle. We'd gone around the block and I'd been pretty scared, though I was just little then.

"He said, 'Well, there's nothing to be scared of,' and he'd give me a call the next day or later that evening—some sort of time he wasn't sure of—and he said, "We're doing night stuff and I'm not sure.' I said he could call me when he wanted to go for a ride and I gave him my number.

"Then he said, 'What's today?' and I said it was almost the end of the day, and he wanted to know when Saturday morning was and I told him. He asked me if I knew where the old castle—a sort of old castlelike building—was in the Hollywood hills, the one gangster Bugsy Siegel had lived in at one time.

"I said I thought I knew but I wasn't sure. He wanted to take a ride up there and look around for things to take pictures of. He said it was by a reservoir, the road went past the reservoir; either way, he said we'd go on an expedition to find it.

"He had my address as well, which I'd written on the back of a page that was an insert for the script, and he didn't call me, but a few days later he showed up on a motorcycle. It was early in the morning—I hadn't been up more than a half hour, and he asked if I was ready to go, as though I'd been sitting there waiting for him.

"I said I was.

"I remember outside he said, 'Don't sit sidesaddle,' and suggested I tuck my skirt between my legs—the part bunched there would hold it down from blowing up.

"We rode up and around Bronson Canyon and when the

road turned to dirt, we rode slowly along it. He was trying to see if he could make out the gangster's castle. He said you could see it on another hill—but he wasn't sure which road led to the place. He said it would be a great place to rent—hidden up in the mountain, and I said he could throw terrific parties. He said he didn't throw parties—he didn't see people—and he said nobody'd come to the parties anyway, which was okay with him.

"He said people were a nuisance and he'd been wanting to find someplace he could rent where he could get away from them. But people tracked him down, he said. They wanted to talk to him or hang around or invite him to parties which he didn't want to go to."

Karen and Jimmy found a little grassy spot between some trees, parked the bike and sat down and to look at the hillsides. After a few moments he asked, "Have you got a boyfriend?"

No, she said, not a steady one. She told him she didn't have someone she was seeing on a regular basis.

"No one special?" he asked.

"I said no. He said, 'Are you playing the field?'

"No, I said. He asked me what I thought of him—James Dean.

"'You're a wonderful actor,' I said. 'You're a nice person—in which way do you mean?'

"He laughed. He'd been smoking and brought out a small plastic bag. He unrolled a marijuana stick and asked, 'You smoke this stuff? I do it because it's bad for you!' He laughed some more." Karen said she told him she'd smoked it a couple times at parties.

He struck a match and lit the reefer, then passed it to her.
She took it without flinching and for a few minutes they passed it back and forth, taking deep drags.

"So I'm a wonderful actor and a nice person," he said, and laughed.

Late at the studio after an all night ride on the motorcycle—"Burning the highway."

"I was just trying to answer your question," she said, and he said, "Am I confusing you? Do you find me a confusing individual?"

"I said, 'No, well maybe not too much—maybe you're confusing me a little.'" He then asked how old she was.

"Boy," he said; he hoped he wasn't robbing the cradle.

She said she was eighteen and he asked her to prove it. Did she have a driver's license? "Do you drive?" he asked.

She showed it to him and said sure she knew how to drive. He looked at her license and asked about her middle name—what it meant; and she told him it was a flower—a flower that is Dutch and grows in Holland. Not a tulip, though.

Then he asked her if she was a virgin. "I laughed and then got embarrassed. I didn't know what to say. He put his arm around me and I said, no, I wasn't a virgin but I wasn't playing the field. He said he wanted to kiss me and I said that would be okay with me.

"He put out the marijuana cigarette, pinching the end and saving it. We kissed for a few minutes and then he asked if I'd ever sucked a guy off. I didn't answer him and he said, 'Well, I guess that's a personal question!'

"I said it sure as shit was—I mean, I *guess*—and we laughed. I asked why he asked me that and he said he was wondering if it was something I'd like.

"'Would you?' I asked. He said, 'Suck someone off or get sucked off?' I said, 'You tell me,' and we kept laughing."

Jimmy cleared his throat almost comically, and said, "Well, let me put it to you another way—how about getting fucked?"

Karen says she asked him if that was the reason he'd brought her up into the hills. He grinned and said, "Yeah!"

It didn't take her long to figure that James Dean was going to try to shock her into submission—testing her in some way; what for, she had no idea. Trying to put her under some kind of microscope.

He said, "I like this sweater you're wearing, too," and he touched it and put his hand on her breast. He said she had beautiful skin. The Aztec priests used to take the skin off people they sacrificed, and they'd have it tanned to wear as cloaks, he told her. "I said he had the weirdest ideas I'd ever heard, and I let him kiss me some more and touch my breasts. He put his hand up under the sweater.

"'When you die,' he told her, 'I could have your skin fixed and wear it—have it tailored into a handsome frock.' He asked me to take off my sweater. I took it off and lay on it because there were sharp pieces of bark in the grass. He kind of curled in against me, moving against me while we kissed. He put his arms around me and whispered for me to remove my panties, and then asked me to unbutton his pants—all the while mostly kissing me. He started moving against me and said, 'Put it in you! Put it in you!' and I sort of rolled on my back and he came over onto me, but we were partly on our sides, and I lifted my leg and sort of put it over his side. We made love on the grass there, and it was done very quickly. He didn't stop kissing or take his arms away from around me."

For all the tactics of shock, Karen says, "Jimmy was gentle and almost docile and he just trembled all over when he had an orgasm, sort of like he was crying. He never put his hands below my waist—just kept holding me and kissing and asking me to do what we had to do to make love.

"After smoking the rest of the marijuana, and while he smoked a cigarette, he said, 'Boy!' and then he looked at his watch. 'Boy oh boy, we got to go. Shit. Fuck!' But he didn't get up.

"He looked at me and said, 'I don't want you to talk to people about our picnic, and that way I'll see you again and we can go out some more.' He said it was really important that people didn't know his business. They were always sticking their noses into his business, and he wanted his business *private*.

"I told him I'd respect that and I understood it. This time on the motorcycle he tucked my skirt between my legs before we took off down the road."

When they got to Karen's, she climbed off and he didn't kill the engine, but asked if she wanted to go to the desert with him. He said he was hiding from some people and wanted to get out of sight. "I asked, 'On the motorcycle?' He said no, in the car. He said he might go the next day or maybe the day after that but he didn't know what they were doing with the schedule, and I said I'd go with him whenever he wanted to go."

14.

Blood and Moonlight

artha Kitt was on the back of Jimmy's bike at three in the morning, wearing a kind of aviatrix helmet. I pulled up alongside on my BSA and I said, "You look like you're ready to fly, lady!"

She said, "Yes! It's French! Isn't it marvelous!" and we all three broke up laughing. She had on tinted glasses, too, a rose shade, and she kept looking around for the moon.

My bike was on Jimmy's right as we rode down Sunset. Eartha had both arms around Jimmy's waist, a little up on his chest, her hands clasped and her face to the side so that her cheekbone was against his shoulder blade.

Near Laurel Canyon, we stopped and talked at the signal by the curb, and then I drove off and Eartha waved good-bye.

Recalling the rides on "that silly motorcycle of Jimmy's," Eartha said, "he scared the devil out of me.... And when I told him that he laughed like a little boy and said 'How can I scare the devil out of the *devil*!'

Eartha told me that sometimes the two of them would go for rides together down Sunset at night. "It was the time he claimed he'd relax," she said. "Twelve—two—three in the morning or later when he'd come over to get me. That was when he liked to ride the most because there were no cars, and he'd say, 'I can think now, when there's no world movement going on around me.' At other times we'd sit on a bus-stop bench and he'd watch whatever little there was going on in the street—he was always watching.... Watching what was happening. What he absorbed was what he observed."

A few nights later I was with Jimmy in the Speedster and he said Jack was driving him crazy. He said he thought Jack would take sleeping pills or cut his wrists. He told me Jack had said some things about me, even though Jimmy'd claimed that he "wasn't interested" in the subject.

This was the night I saw Bill Smith on La Cienega at Melrose. Bill's sister had been an actress, and Bill was doggedly chasing a career of his own—years later he'd star with Clint Eastwood in *Any Which Way You Can*. I introduced Bill to Jimmy, who did not get out but reached across the passenger side to shake his hand. Jimmy said, "Nice to meet you," and then giggled a little and made some sort of face about Bill's forceful grip.

I got out and Bill said, "I love this car...." I went into a liquor store for cigarettes while Jimmy waited at the curb. When I came out, Jimmy had the hood open and they were standing at the rear of the car looking at the engine. I remember Jimmy nodding and Bill saying something about having worked on a Volkswagen engine, but never having seen a Porsche's. We got back in and Bill bent down by my side of the car, saying he was glad to have met Jimmy. When we drove off, Jimmy chuckled and said, "So that's the guy with the hard-on."

I said yeah, to which Jimmy said, "What if he showed it to

you now? What would you do now?" I said I didn't think he'd do that.

"That wasn't what I asked you," Jimmy said. "I said what would you do?"

"Nothing," I said.

Jimmy said, "We both know what Jack would do." I said he wouldn't wait until Bill showed it to him, but I was sure Jack wouldn't survive to blab about the attempt. Jimmy laughed. He took my hand and put it on his crotch and said, "What if he did this?" He said he'd bet Bill wouldn't do something like that. He imagined Bill was all muscle without a whole lot "sparking between his ears." If Bill jacked off with the same strength he'd shown in shaking Jimmy's hand, he said his cock was probably carried around in a sling. Jimmy had his hand around my left wrist and held my hand on his crotch as he drove, moving both our hands to the shifter when he put in the clutch, guiding us into gear and saying, "Hey, I'm teaching you to drive, man."

Rebel Without a Cause, directed by Nick Ray, would be a considerable box-office success, though *New York Herald Tribune* critic William K. Zinsser said, "The movie is written and acted so ineptly, directed so sluggishly, that all names but one will be omitted….The exception is Dean, the gifted young actor….His rare talent and appealing personality shine through even this turgid melodrama."

Once again Dean played a troubled youth, again struggling to communicate with an unfeeling father. He portrayed a new student in a L.A. high school, where he encounters violence and meets two other misunderstood teenagers, portrayed by Natalie Wood and Sal Mineo.

"Working in *Rebel* was like being part of a close-knit family," says Sal Mineo. "I've never experienced it in any other film. Everybody became very tight, and Jimmy was the focus

Sal Mineo worshipped Jimmy on the *Rebel* set, but was afraid to "talk to him as a person...."

of it. We all grew around him, and as a result we all tended to idolize him. At first I was afraid of him, I was terrified of him. I really didn't know him at all, but I worshiped the way he dealt with people in a higher position. He'd never take anything from anybody, never take any nonsense from them no matter what the situation was.

"I never thought of him as being unfeeling. I did feel there was something behind some of his actions that other people might call cruel or unsympathetic to others—I mean things like there were mornings when he really was awful to people, he'd totally disregard them and not say anything the whole day, and a man could feel rejected and I'd end up saying, 'What did I do wrong?' I was very impressionable. I was only sixteen, and if he didn't say good morning to me I'd be a wreck the whole day.

"But if he put his arm around me, that was fabulous, because then I knew he meant it. I always felt he was just testing people, testing to see how far he could push.

"The day I got killed in the film was a very important day for me. The scene was that I ran out of the planetarium and got shot, and Jimmy discovers me dead and hovers over me, and expresses what he feels at the moment. So he had a number of choices to make.

"Now here was the chance for me to feel what it would be like for someone close, someone that I idolized, to be grieving for me. It was an opportunity to experience what kind of grief that would be—what would he be like, what would he sound like, what would he be thinking?

"And I wanted to do that scene over and over again, and each time we did it, he'd position me in the kind of repose that would work best for him to get the emotion going. It was very moving for me, because he was very moved. When you see the finished scene you can see how he broke up at the moment that was used in the film.

"Immediately after the scene, I noticed there was a change in the relationship—he was very protective, and for the whole day he'd never let me out of his sight. He was always there."

Like Sal Mineo, Natalie Wood, too, felt guided by Jimmy during the filming of the picture. It was her first break from the good-girl, child-actress category, and the intimate scenes with Jimmy were the first love scenes she would play.

"The thing that strikes me about Jimmy now," Natalie said later, "is that at the time he seemed like the great nonconformist, a great rebel, but really he was only eccentric then, and he wouldn't be considered wild by today's standards.

"We used to go to lunch on his motorcycle to a nearby hamburger joint when we were doing a television show after *Rebel*, and he was fascinated about the stories that were being written

Natalie Wood: "I had a crush on Jimmy that wouldn't quit, but he treated me like I was still six years old."

about him. He was trying hard to figure out how he was being seen by others."

Meanwhile, Jack volunteered to me some ambiguous statements about his closeness to Jimmy, hinting at sex—"I won't say yes and I won't say no," he chirped. Even then, he claimed that he both loved and worshiped Jimmy, but that they were "friends first."

It was bewildering to many, the importance Jack had to Jimmy, over and above any of the members of the *Rebel* cast. Before the film started, Jimmy had even suggested to Nick Ray that Jack play Sal Mineo's role, and had Jack tested for the

He banged around the Warner Bros. lot, earning the title "that little bastard!"

part, though Jack, being not nearly as experienced an actor as Sal, would certainly have had a difficult time with it.

The test was shot one night on location during a break for another setup. I'd ridden over with Jack in the hearse. It was the scene in the mansion with Sal and Natalie Wood.

When we got there, Jimmy walked past her, then reached and put his hand under the front of her skirt. She jerked up because he'd pinched her thigh. She said, "Damn it! I asked you not to *pinch* me like that!"

That night, tension developed between Jack and Jimmy and myself. After the filming, Jack drove me to Hamburger Hamlet on the Strip, where we would later be met by Jimmy and Rolf Wutherich. They drove over in Jimmy's Speedster, at moments hitting seventy miles an hour along Sunset.

Jimmy drank milk at Hamburger Hamlet. He didn't smoke that night, complaining about a sore throat. The two of us talked about bikes for a while and Jack hardly spoke. After Jimmy left for his apartment on Sunset Plaza Drive, Jack said Jimmy'd told him that he'd met me in New York through James Sheldon—which wasn't accurate. I said I'd met Sheldon through Jimmy. That was the end of the conversation, though Jack wanted me to come to his place that night and talk to him. I said I couldn't. I had an interview first thing in the morning and I wanted to get to sleep. He asked me to meet him and Maila at Googie's the next day and I said I'd call him, or talk to Jimmy. That upset him.

For days, Jack kept calling me and trying in every way he could to get me to talk about Jimmy and New York. Everything he said seemed to be an attempt to pry out some information about anything sexual that might have happened between Jimmy and myself.

A girl who'd lost a leg in a motorcycle accident was coming in and out of Googie's, and said she really wanted to meet James Dean. She knew he liked talented and unusual people, and he wasn't a phony like so many other movie and television assholes she claimed to know.

The girl was sitting at the counter, looking right at him and smiling. He said, "You see that girl? She's a nice girl. She's only got one leg." She was also singing in clubs on the Strip, would later write an autobiography in which she described a scene of Jimmy coming to her apartment and asking her to strip naked, which she did. Jimmy stared at her body and he told her how beautiful she was. He then touched her skin with his fingers, and felt and kissed her stump.

One night Jimmy wanted to meet Samson DeBrier, a Hollywood "character" and actor, rumored to have been the homosexual lover to André Gide, author of *The Immoralist*.

We rode our bikes to Samson's house, Jimmy weaving in and out of Sunset Boulevard traffic. When he'd hit a straight pitch, he'd take his hands off the grips and pull at his glove or fool around with his glasses.

Samson's house was a museum of pirated movie relics and antique set decorations, and he usually held an "open house," a kind of revolving party. Kenneth Anger's film *Inauguration of the Pleasure Dome*, had been filmed in the house, with DeBrier, Anaïs Nin, and experimental filmmaker Curtis Harrington playing parts, and Jimmy was eager to meet and talk to Samson. He knew about Harrington's experimental films; we'd talked about *Fragment of Seeking*. Jimmy was hoping to meet with Harrington as well.

Among the people there that night was another young and struggling actor I'd seen around town, a nice guy named Jack Nicholson, from New Jersey. He was all smiles when he saw Jimmy, and at one point he cornered me, first asking where I'd bought the motorcycle jacket, and what "we" were riding. He asked me to introduce him to Jimmy, who was talking to Samson in the kitchen.

I said to Jimmy, "This is Jack Nicholson," and Jack

reached out his hand but Jimmy mumbled something and turned back to face Samson. The snub had nothing to do with Jack personally—it was something Jimmy did—but Jack was embarrassed. I made some excuse, telling him it was the wind and the bikes that did something to Jimmy's eyes and ears. I said it was a "noise and visual factor."

Jack nodded and turned to a cute girl standing at his side. He never let on that he'd been bothered by Jimmy's snubbing him, though in the instant it had happened I could see him caving in right in front of me.

Jimmy rarely socialized with other actors, especially members of the *Rebel* cast—not even Natalie Wood and director Nick Ray. He was not friendly or on talking terms with other Warner contract players like Sal Mineo or Dennis Hopper. In time, Sal would be one of the few to publicly state his distance from Jimmy, while still desiring to have been closer in any way possible. Following Jimmy's death, others like Dennis Hopper and Nick Adams would not be able to resist fabricating personal friendships with Jimmy, frienship that had little to do with real life.

Just a week or so before that night, I'd been bopping along with Jimmy toward the Warner Brothers commissary and Sal Mineo was up ahead of us. Jimmy sneaked up behind him and pinched him on the right cheek of his ass. Sal jumped, startled, his big brown eyes wide as cake plates. His face flushed red when he saw it was Jimmy, and then he giggled which started Jimmy laughing. Sal's face beamed with admiration and awe.

One afternoon at the commissary, Dean confronted a giant blow-up picture of himself. He pulled it down from the wall, and carried it like a flag to the table where Ted Ashton and a few of the publicity people were lunching.

Jimmy ripped the picture in half and threw the pieces on the table. He said, "Don't ever put my fucking picture up in here! Whatta you think, that I live here or something? You think you own me? Nobody owns me!"

Another time I used Jimmy's camera and took pictures of him and Dennis Hopper, under contract to Warner, and playing in *Rebel*. Jimmy had said, "This guy keeps following me around." In one picture, Jimmy was holding a skull to his face, as if to whisper in its ear, while Dennis in the background raised a sort of Arabian broadsword as if he were about to attack some outsider on the scene.

Once Jimmy said, "If I get in a room by myself for a while I feel like I can take a break and I don't have to present myself to somebody." His "movie star" abode was something like that—a furnished apartment over Sunset, one room with a kitchen, littered with paper cups and take-out orders from drive-ins and Googie's, plus stacks of papers and spools of recording tape and his clothes, the latter thrown carelessly into the closet. He'd scoop up some shirts and pants from a chair, open the little closet's partitioned door like a folding screen, and throw the clothes in on top of whatever else was there.

Once after calling me to come up the hill, he was eating sardines and leaning against the sink, looking sick. After a while he said, "You know, any kind of pain is a sort of misdirected energy. You know that? When your finger hurts, it's because you got it banged because you weren't directed. It's the same with pains in the stomach and in the head, which is stress and tension—misdirected energy, it can cause all the sicknesses there are."

A cuff link lay on the floor with some some shirt buttons and pair of brown boots with the left sole coming unstitched from the shoe. This was Dean's apartment as he attempted to direct his energies, a space littered with bullfighting practice pants, scuffed-up boots, a Webcor tape recorder, and Jimmy— listening to a drum section he'd recorded with Cyril Jackson in New York. He'd bought a conga drum similar to the one Brando used. Hanging on the wall by the door was an old black leather motorcycle jacket—almost identical to the one Brando wore in *The Wild One*. On the bed was another leather jacket which wasn't horsehide and had a snap flap at the collar.

Whenever I was there, I usually made coffee and he'd drink it down fast; sometimes he seemed to swill it right down though it was really hot. He'd make one phone call after another, and sometimes he'd say almost the same things to different people, or he'd giggle on the phone and want to know what someone thought of him and about what he was doing.

I remember it like this: He took his shoes off, pushed them off, and the toe section of one sock was torn through. I knew that somewhere in the room he'd stashed a quite a bit of cash, maybe wadded into a box somewhere or an old envelope like the kind scripts are mailed in. Once when he was staying at the studio, he carried more than a thousand dollars stuffed down inside his sock.

So he was on the phone and he looked at his toe abstractedly, wiggled it, then gradually crossed his leg and pulled off the sock and threw it toward the wastebasket. Then he was up, pacing and pulling on the phone cord as he talked, now hushed tones, the next moment laughing.

"No," he said. "Someone's here, fuck no, what're you, crazy?" Later on he was talking to Karen Davis because I could hear her crying and it was almost an electrical screech coming through.

Soon he was laughing and she wasn't crying, and he took the phone into the bathroom where he sat on the toilet. Shirts and towels were piled around, some smudged with makeup, some wet. There was a copy of the script of *Rebel* in the bathtub; he said he'd skim through it and make notes for ideas on directing.

He was making another phone call, complaining about how he didn't want to do something because it would make him seem as if he were doing it for some other reason than it being something he wanted to do. That wasn't right, he said. "I'd just go around regretting it forever and forever and it will come back to me and I'll have nightmares over it."

Whenever he did sleep, it was like someone thinking of the answer to a difficult question, but one that was funny, too, because his slightly opened lips would jerk nervously at the corners of his mouth, a tugging upward into a smile, and his eyebrows would lift inquiringly. Or his eyes would open a little if he turned his head to the side, and I'd think he was awake, but he was sleeping with his eyes open and the irises were dull-looking—the lids half hiding the corneas.

He was asleep on his side with his knees drawn up midway and with those hands clasped between his thighs as if he was trying to keep them warm. Once or twice a hand would flex in his crotch, the fingers pressing against his cock. They'd flex and jerk slightly the same as when he'd pull at the corners of his mouth. He laughed a few times and then he said, "No, that's not now, that's not going to go that way—" and he gave a questioning yank of the brows.

Then he opened his eyes and was sitting up in the same position, the same movement, as though he hadn't slept at all, and was just rising to reach out for the phone.

When he did want to rest, he would lie back and start to listen to something or he'd be on the phone and as soon as he'd hang it up he seemed to go to sleep. He did this with his clothes on and lying on top of the sheet, or else the bed was askew and rumpled as if the maid hadn't been there to clean it, the bottom of the sheet across the bed dirty from his boots.

There were moments when he reminded me of the dead guy he'd seen in the cop wagon back in New York. Jimmy was really unlike any kind of movie actor I'd ever known. On the bed he looked small—like a child refugee from some sort of war.

Rosen would later prove right about him: He wasn't like Greta Garbo. Jimmy didn't want to be alone. Maybe he *couldn't* be alone. I was quickly learning that he didn't know how to live in a place. He was more like a kind of animal. He didn't know how to *have* a place of his own.

He didn't know how to live with himself.

15.

Guts

When I told Jimmy about the ting-a-ling guy he was enraptured. "The coolest cat I've ever come across," I said. We'd been talking horses, where he'd stabled Cisco, what he was planning on doing. The discussion turned to Pickwick stables in Burbank, and I told him about Sleepy Hollow stables south of Griffith Park where I used to ride every week. I had a horse—not my own—a fast quarter pony named Night Song, that'd been my favorite.

My stepbrother and I used to hitch rides from the stables to Burbank, along Riverside Drive out of L.A. One night a guy pulled up in a chopped Model A rod without a hood, running stacked with dual cards. He was wearing tea-timer shades and a black leather jacket and said, "You cats want a lift?"

Hey, sure—and in we piled, me first, a tight squeeze with my stepbrother on my right. The door shut and the guy peeled out, laying rubber all the way across the intersection onto Riverside Drive, hitting seventy or better in seconds and then

Backing the speedster out of the Sunset Plaza driveway.

backed off a little, that engine howling like a bobcat. I remember "How High the Moon" playing—Les Paul and Mary Ford. The guy looked over with a smile. He said, "You cats play ting-a-ling?"

Play what?

"Ting-a-ling," he said. "On the road, man...." His pompadour stood as high as his forehead, stiff with some kind of wave set.

Ting-a-ling? No—what's that?

"Oh, man," he said, "what you've been *missssing!* Point's to blow a bumper a kiss, man, get a little feel of the steel, you dig? You hep to this jive I'm putting down?"

No—we weren't.

He was shaking his head sadly. "Show you how it works. You see that broad ass up front of us, a-blinkin' and winkin'?" He meant a big Buick ahead of us, less than a quarter mile, the red taillights bright and dimming—bright and dimming. The guy was nervous on the brake or didn't know he was riding it. "The point of the action's to sneak up a little on her, and give her a little kiss—a little ting-a-ling."

What was he talking about?

He said, "Can't hardly explain, man, to give it its dues, so let me show you how it goes...."

Wham! Still smiling, he threw that short, chopped-down gearshift hard, his feet jumping at the clutch and gas, and the little rod sort of stood up on its hind end with the wheels burning the asphalt.

We lunged ahead like one of those tigers in the cartoons where their back legs turn into whirring propellers. The momentum sucked our backs into the seat.

Then he killed the lights! Was he nuts? "Got to sneak up, man, or she'll jump ship—" He was racing without lights straight at the rear of the Buick as if to climb right over it or collide with such force we'd crush into one mashed chunk.

"Roll it down!" he said. "Roll it down, man!" He meant the window. My stepbrother was white-faced and stiff on the seat, his face so stretched with fear it looked like his eyes would fall out. I reached past him and rolled the dinky window down and the air hit us like out of a wind tunnel.

By then we'd hit eighty-five or ninety, and he jammed into third, thromped the gas, and went back into a lower gear as the Buick's back jumped straight up at us.

But the engine screeched, he jerked to the left, swerving at the same time so sharp past the Buick, the right tip of his custom bumper struck the rear left curving end of the Buick's and made a quick clang—a sliding-steel pinging noise as we swerved past and into the lane of oncoming traffic, with such a breakneck jerking speed our lower jaws felt pulled back from the rest of our heads.

Oncoming headlights actually veered right as he sailed around the Buick—way ahead of it—and then eased down into the right lane.

"Well—well," he said with a satisfied smile. "You dig that little sound, man? That's how you play ting-a-ling." After a moment he said, "You can roll that glass back up, it's a little chilly, don't you think?"

Jimmy said he was too low in the Porsche. He couldn't do that—he'd slide right under. "Maybe we can do it on the bike?"

"The bike?" I asked.

"Yeah! Do it on the bike—connecting in some way with the rear bumper as you get around it. Shit! What a trick, man. That's *got* to be done."

He tried to talk Nick Ray into working a scene into *Rebel* with a little ting-a-ling action. But Nick said he couldn't fit it in. He said it seemed too "antisocial" and would cast an unsympathetic light on the characters participating in such a stunt.

But Jimmy persisted and talked about it with Stewart Stern who just stared at Jimmy with a stricken look. "There's no justification or rationale in the story for including something like that," Stewart said. "The mere idea is terrifying."

Nick told Jimmy it would be censored everywhere. "Stewart's brought it up and, frankly, apart from the bad implications, it'd cost a lot and nobody'd see it. Forget it."

Jimmy told me, "Stewart's got problems, you know. We talked about art—he told me about a story he'd written and it was absolutely brilliant but he's afraid to let anybody see it. He's afraid of exposure—of showing he has guts instead of Peter Pan stuffing."

Later Stewart said, "He had these ideas to shock people—violence for the sake of being violent. When carried to some logical conclusion, if something like he was suggesting can ever be logical, it's too dangerous for innocent people— ruthless bravado for its own sake. It represents a disdain for life, for others on the road as well as one's own life. "

When Brando heard about the ting-a-ling idea, through Stewart, he said, "No one in their right mind does such a thing. It's a criminal act—willful, and jeopardizing innocent lives. It's merely a reflection of the recklessness Dean exhibits that everyone's afraid of. And the fact that he's subscribing to these acts of creating fear in others, we're right back to getting him to a psychiatrist as quickly as possible."

Eartha Kitt says, "Most of all he was like that small boy jumping off the back-porch steps, who keeps jumping and then hopping and then he graduates to running across the street and darting in and out of the traffic..."

A few days later, Jimmy screwed up his left leg and asked me not to say anything to anyone in case it got back to "some asshole" in the studio. How he did it stuck in my mind like a barb on a wire.

A couple times we'd taken off on the bikes to get him over the hill to Warners. Nobody knew he was a movie star and he'd crank the hell out of it heading north on Highland once getting off Franklin and away from the boulevard. I was falling back with the feeling that if I just turned off somewhere, like before hitting the Cahuenga Freeway over the hill (this was 101), that he'd wind up in Burbank, cruising in cool at the gate, and not even thinking that he'd left me somewhere back on the highway.

He went to the left—sharp—jerked in front of a car that blew its horn and he threw back his right hand, giving the finger. I don't know that he cared whether there was any highway patrol guys on the road or not. I have to look back at that and wonder whether he really gave it any serious thought. I know I did. I was always sort of chickenshit of getting jammed with another speeding ticket.

What he did with his left leg happened after he'd sailed over Cahuenga and turned north on Barham Boulevard, called "the pass," up over the hill bordering Universal City, and then headed down the long grade into Burbank. Down at the bottom of the hill was a stop sign where Riverside Drive joined the pass—a connecting, T-intersection.

I'd let the engine ride down, going into a lower gear when approaching the bottom so I wouldn't have to jam it to a stop. Jimmy was way ahead of me, and while I was slowing, the distance between us kept stretching farther. He wasn't letting up on the gas but was riding it open—he wasn't slowing down.

A couple cars heading west on Riverside Drive stopped at the sign across the lane and then proceeded ahead onto Barham. It looked to me like Jimmy was going to hit the grade hard and jump the stop sign—just plow through.

I lost sight for a moment because of a car on my right and it went to the left lane, and then as I came around it, I saw the smoke of Jimmy burning his tire as he braked at the bottom of the hill. His bike was skidding to the right, sort of out from under him but he held it and went with it, and he was sort of hopping on that left leg to stay with it. The car he'd almost broadsided had swerved right, cut sharp, and slowed until Jimmy'd braked the bike to a stop—the engine dead.

As I pulled to the right, Jimmy was quickly uprighting the bike and pushing it east of the intersection, going diagonally onto Riverside Drive. His face was white and he was sweating around the eyes. He was swearing like mad and said he'd popped his left knee, knocked it out of joint and then jumped it back in.

He stood the bike and then squatted down, holding his

knee and rocking himself in pain. I didn't know what I could do for him. He asked me to get his bike running and I started it up and let it rev a little. I said it was okay. He was in pain but he didn't say anything and I didn't go on the lot with him that day. At the gate he told me not to say anything.

I rode to a girl's place down Alameda in Burbank. She'd been a high-school whore and we used to go ice-skating at the Polar Palace in Hollywood, sometimes with Joby Baker, another kid actor also a friend of Charlie Bronson's. Once or twice we'd seen Charlie by Paramount—which was just across from the Polar Palace. Joby'd get a big break with Spencer Tracy in *The Last Angry Man*.

I felt strange and kind of sick to my stomach that day, a sort of wiggly sense of something seriously wrong.

The girl and I made out for a while. She was afraid of getting pregnant so I fucked her in the ass using some Dixie Peach hair pomade. After that, we drank Coke and smoked, and I told her about what had happened on the pass, and how I felt funny, maybe even like part of a piece of machinery—I could've been a taillight or a handgrip or a section of pipe as far as having any controlling measure as to what'd happened, or what could've happened if he hadn't braked in time and that car hadn't jolted to the right.

She said I had to tell him something about what I felt. That I had the sense that speeding like that was wrong and it was going to lead to some serious consequences.

I knew she was right but I also knew I'd never say something like that.

People were hounding Jimmy, trying to get close to him— holding him in awe. There were times when Googie's was packed because most of them wanted to see Jimmy Dean in action. Still there were people who, holding him in awe, would not approach him, nor would they make an effort to get close to him. There were two people I can recall, one a young boy I knew, the other an older person, neither of whom wanted to get near him—but just a look through the glass partition to the back area of Googie's. That was the extent of it. The boy said he'd be afraid to get to know him closely because he might "take away who I am."

We'd hang out in Googie's new back patio, crowded with tables, chairs, rubber plants, and a palm tree that reached up and peeked through an opening in the fiberglass roof, which was like a covering over a carport.

One night he wasn't there and Karen Davis made her way into the rear. Jimmy had talked about her—he'd invited me to come up one night when she was at his place and take her home. He'd said she loved to ride on the bike. "Take her for a ride."

I hadn't been able to tell right off what the situation between Jimmy and Karen was about. That night she said, "You're with Jimmy a lot, but you're not working at Warners." I said I wasn't, that I'd been with him in New York a couple years back. She said, "Are you gay?"

I said, "No, I'm not particularly gay—why, are you?"

"Is Jimmy gay?" she asked.

"Not particularly gay—" I said.

"That's your stock answer to the question, I see."

"Well, I'm not going to say what he is. I mean you work it out for yourself."

"But you're around him here—"

"So?"

"I'm trying to understand him."

"Good luck," I said.

Later on Karen called me at my mother's where I was staying. She wanted to meet me. When I showed up she told me she thought she was pregnant. She was in love with Jimmy and told me she thought he was trying to kill himself.

She said he'd hit her because she was pushing the relationship. "He hit me a couple of times—I wanted him to tell me he loves me…. Instead, we're getting into fights.

"Other times we neck and go on necking," she said, "and nothing else…. Now we're getting really platonic and he wants to play games."

She said she loved Jimmy's skin—that he had a beautifully smooth boy's body; his skin was very soft and smooth to touch. "I rub my fingers up and down his back," she said, "and he just lays there on his stomach."

During one of their last times together she said, Jimmy came to her place, sat down and looked at her and started crying. When she tried to comfort him, to put her arms around him and hold him and tell him it was okay, he threw her arms off and stormed out. "That was it," she said. "And I haven't told him I might be pregnant."

She said a while back he'd taken her on the bike and raced through Laurel Canyon and down into the valley—"going much faster than he was able to control the thing," she insisted.

Finally, she said, he ran it against the side of the road and bent the front forks.

It was just an accident, I said, he'd told me about it. But she was sure it wasn't. "He wants to die, and he's too chicken to do it himself so he's going to take someone with him."

"Bullshit," I said.

Two weeks later, when *Rebel* was finished and Jimmy was on his way to Texas to star in *Giant* with Elizabeth Taylor, Karen told me that Jimmy was sending her back to New York, paying her way and even getting her a "great apartment" on Fifty-eighth Street. Much later on, she was to tell me: "I was very hurt by Jimmy not wanting to make more of what we had, because I thought he didn't care about me. He said he had these problems—it wasn't that he didn't want to have more to do with me, just that he couldn't get involved with anyone. 'I don't want to have anyone that I have to depend on,' she said.

It was some time later that I heard another version of the New York travel story.

According to Sol Rosen, Jimmy met briefly with Karen before he left on location, and told her he wasn't opposed to her being pregnant. He told me he'd said to her, "If you want, you can have the baby. We can be together with it, we can be living together but I don't want to get married."

Karen wanted to know if he'd thought about marrying her if she had the baby. He said he told her that was a possibility but it was something he wasn't in any position to make a decision about at that point in his life.

"You want to live together," she said, "only because I'm pregnant, but you're not sure if we can get married and give the baby a name?"

"We can name the baby," he said. "There's nothing illegal about a baby getting a name even though its parents aren't married. Hell, it's going to have a legal birth certificate." Or, Jimmy supposedly said to her, "If you don't want to have the baby and you want to get something done, then we can work that out, too." She wanted to know what he meant and he said it could be worked out financially. He'd talk to someone.

Her question was whether Jimmy loved her or not, and he said he told her he didn't love her. "I like you a lot," he said, "but I'm not in love with you—I don't love anyone," he said. "It's not a fair thing for us to be talking about that as it hasn't got much to do with having a baby—whether the people that've done it are in love or not." She said it did to her.

"Well," he said, "what can we do about that?"

She said she'd have to make a decision what to do about it. She said, "What would the studio do about it?"

Jimmy said he thought it over and told her he wasn't sure

what they'd suggest and did she want him to bring it up with someone?

She said he might as well so they could consider any other options that were part of the situation.

The first person he talked to was Elbers, the studio troubleshooter. Elbers said, "What does she want to do?"

"I don't know for sure. She said she wants to consider options."

"Does she want money?" Elbers asked.

"I don't know. Should I give her money—what for? To get it taken care of? For support of the baby or something? Sheez, I said I'd have her come and live with me and she could have the baby."

"No, that's not going to work, Jimmy," Elbers told him. "We'll talk to Sol Rosen and see what he thinks."

The first thing Rosen wanted to know was how did she know it was Jimmy's?

"Maybe she figures I'm the only person she's been with in that period of time."

"That's what she might say but how does one know?"

He shrugged. "I told her she could live with me."

"That's impossible. Jesus—you can't even live with yourself."

Jimmy laughed.

Sol said, "I'll think this out and call you later today."

"Well, I didn't call him later but I called him earlier," Sol says. "I gave it a couple of minutes of thought and began to see what a complication it could become in a short time until the thing was nipped in the bud. It was a sure cinch that it was something Jimmy wasn't going to be able to fool around with—he was leaving for Texas in a matter of days, as soon as he'd finished some synching on *Rebel*.

"I asked him who she was and how I could talk to her and

he gave me her phone number and her address, and where she was working.

"What I did, I drove over to the beauty parlor and asked her if she could take a break and we might have some coffee to discuss the problem.

"She said it certainly was a problem.

"We went to a restaurant and she had lunch and I asked her what she wanted. She said Jimmy told her he was going to Texas and she said she'd like to go there.

"I explained how impossible that would be with a George Stevens picture. She asked what the possibilities were for her to get a part in a picture—one of Jimmy's pictures that would be coming up in the near future?

"I said the possibility was good. I said we could guarantee her television work in New York, and an apartment if she was agreeable to that."

"'New York?'"

"I nodded. 'New York. At least until this situation has been decided one way or another by you—and by Jimmy.'"

"'What about finances?'" she asked.

"I told her that could be taken care of.

"She asked, 'How much?'

"I said we'd have to discuss that. Negotiate it. 'We're keeping this very low-level right now. No one really knows about it and I'd hate for it to get to the front office right at this time because I know they'd refute the situation.'

"'What do you mean "refute it"?'"

"'Deny that it is Jimmy you're pregnant by. I mean, there's isn't any proof as it stands, and it could get to be a real waste of everyone's energies and finances.'

"She didn't say anything, and I quickly put in that this sort of thing happens. I said, 'There was an extra a couple of weeks ago who said she was pregnant by Jimmy—that her boyfriend hadn't had sex with her but she'd had it with

Jimmy. It went to the front office and she was proved to be lying, so Warner Brothers is preparing to take legal action against her. Do you have any idea how much a movie like *Giant* could cost in damages if something delayed the production?'

"Karen said, 'I have no intention for something like that. That's the furthest thing from my mind.'

"'That's a relief,' I said. 'For all of us. But let me put it this way: If you're willing to take a break from your claims on Jimmy, and try to get yourself ahead in your career, with our assistance I think you will surely be in a position to survey the situation with a clear, objective point of view.'

"She said she understood. Then she offered, 'Jimmy says he isn't in love with me. He says he doesn't love anyone.'

"'You should know that's true,' I said. 'He's an ego-maniac.'

"She laughed. 'Nobody's ever said that, but it is true. What happens if I go ahead and have the baby and it looks just like Jimmy?'

"I looked very serious. 'Let's talk about that when we get to that bridge. I'd suggest you not have the baby, unless you've got some reason why you couldn't go through with—having the problem taken care of.'

"'Maybe....' she said. 'Maybe we'll see what happens. I should talk to Jimmy about all this—'

"'No,' I said, cutting in on her. 'We're talking about it now. He can't talk about this. What's he going to say that he hasn't already said?'

"'I know,' she said, wistfully. 'He doesn't want to get married.'

"'That can't be forced without a fight,' I said. 'You're far better off to be opportunistic in this situation. Look at the bright side. You're too intelligent a girl to deliberately court disaster.'"

. . .

"Did I scare her? I don't know," Sol says. "I tried to scare her. I tried to put the fear of God into her to make her see we're a lot bigger than she is. She wasn't a hard-ass. She was a pretty girl—cute, bright. I could see she was soft—motherly. Would've made a good mother."

But she didn't make up her mind. Instead she contacted Jimmy again and went to his place and sat outside. He spotted her car and turned around, heading back down to Sunset. He drove another few blocks and stayed at Jack's.

He told Jack something about it and Jack was the one who then intervened, telling her that the studio was restricting him from seeing her and he'd be suspended if he saw her without the studio's approval. The only way that could be arranged was between her attorneys and Warner Brothers.

She said she didn't have an attorney. Jack said, "So what's the fight? Take a break and get a trip to New York. Get some work on television—you can be just like Jimmy—get work and go onstage, and look out for your own independent career. Let Warner Brothers help you find that for yourself... and come back and be a movie star!"

16.

A Dangerous Streak

"Why should we shed maudlin tears and slobber over the memory of James Dean?" asked show-business biographer Maurice Zolotow. "What's so great and beautiful about stepping on the gas, blowing your horn and speeding down a public highway like a maniac? To some extent, what our country will become tomorrow is determined by whom our children admire today."

Sammy Davis, Jr., answered: "I don't give a fuck how some of these assholes criticize Dean. He did his number and he did it better than anybody else in the world!"

Davis met Jimmy in a nightclub shortly before the summer. "We were beating bongo drums till two in the morning," Davis said. "I said we had to do it some more, had to connect real soon. I was living with my grandmother at the time, and invited Jimmy to come to the house. Once he showed up in the middle of the afternoon and picked up the lid from the pot my granny was cooking a roast in. He quoted some line from

Milton's *Paradise Lost* and stood there breathing in the steam until his glasses got all fogged over."

Looking back, Davis said, "There's a lot of jealousy about Jimmy, *a lot* of jealousy in terms of why should he have all this admiration? Why should people still have a kind of thing about him all these years after he's passed?

"Well, there are only two people in the world that I can remember within my lifetime creating that thing. One was Marilyn Monroe and the other was James Dean."

Eartha Kitt was more specific: "It's amazing how one body like that can have such an impact on the world. And I think it frightened him. Jimmy wanted to be the biggest thing in the world, he wanted to be a man of quality, but he was very frightened of the business, frightened of the things that were going on around him....

"He was really very weak in a certain way you couldn't know unless you knew him well, and out of that weakness he thought he might do something rash. He was afraid of it, if ever he got to a point where he might not be able to handle things. I think he was frightened of dying but drawn to conquer that fear in himself."

One night Jimmy called me to say he was switching out engines in the Triumph. Getting a bigger, more powerful Triumph engine. "What are you doing?" he asked. He wanted to know if I'd ride down to Santa Monica with him to the bike shop—bring him back after he left his bike there.

He said, "I got to just ride and blow some of the shit out of my head."

On the way down we stopped at a coffee shop on Lincoln Boulevard and he told me about heading down to Texas with Elizabeth Taylor. He said, "She's really nice, man. She's sweet and she's got tits that won't quit." He told me about the lights hitting her and she seemed to bathe in them "like she's phosphorous or something," and her skin seemed to still radiate the light when they'd extinguished. "She kissed me," he said.

"Oh yeah?" I said.

"I asked her, 'What're you giving me a kiss for?'" Jimmy said, "and she said, 'It's a secret.' I asked her, 'What's the secret?'—I wanted to share in this secret. She said she'll tell me someday soon. I said, 'What's the matter with today?' and she laughed—this sort of mellow hee-haw laugh—and I figure it's got to be something pretty funny. But she says no, it's not anything funny. She said, 'You want me to tell you right now and that'd ruin the secret.' I said, 'Shucks no, I got secrets too, secrets are good to have,' I said. They're like ammunition. I said to her, 'You got secrets that're like ammunition?'

"She said, 'Oh, oh, oh,' and that she doesn't need any ammunition. 'I can see why he says he thinks you're in need of ammunition—'

Jimmy said Liz meant George Stevens. He said, "I'm getting second thoughts about this man. Kind of like waiting for the king of the world, like waiting for Christ or God to come out of heaven and the fucker's digging out toejam with a toothpick."

Jack Simmons spent two weeks reading to Jimmy all of Edna Ferber's novel, which the script had been based upon. Jimmy said he had "a different perspective" on the character of Jett Rink—the one he was playing, than what he was getting from Stevens. The character was based on a "real, rough-and-tumble oil boomer who comes from dirt," Jimmy said, "and hits it so rich he's in the driver's seat of those that've looked down on him." On that, Jimmy and the director agreed, but how to interpret that was a different matter and they didn't agree.

As if hiding, Jimmy couldn't be reached at the Sunset Plaza phone, and had dumped half of his things at Jack

Simmons' in Hollywood. Jack worshiped Jimmy: he'd enshrined a pair of Jimmy's old scuffed boots in plastic, and plastered one wall of the apartment with stills from *Eden* and *Rebel.*

As he had in *Rebel*, Jimmy got Jack a part in a television show in which he was appearing. For Jimmy, the show proved a shining light in the mud of the moment. But again he was faced with opposition.

Former president Ronald Reagan, then hosting and appearing on television's *General Electric Theater*, said he was "disgusted by Dean's 'hep cat' attitude and insolent manner." Though the show was one of the season's best efforts, Reagan tried to have the segment he worked in with Jimmy canned.

"I hate that kind of person—what Dean represents," Reagan told an associate producer. "I hate this kind of New York school of acting—this 'dirty shirt' school of acting as it's called. It should be outlawed along with this rock-and roll-recording business. I'm trying to have the whole sour episode shelved. Nothing would please me more if we can have it burned."

Jimmy was calling Eartha Kitt as well during preproduction on *Giant*. "Pretty soon," she said, "we'd be getting into these long talks across the country from Texas after he went on location. The studio had restricted him from entering any races, and even from speeding a motorcycle around studio property.

"He'd call me in New York where I'd gone for [a] play, and he'd keep me up half the night getting into deep feelings about his discomfort with the film.

"Always, he said, he'd thought of George Stevens as a kind of 'king of the mountain,' seconded only by Kazan, since Stevens made *A Place in The Sun*, but Stevens was now more inclined to go along with Rock Hudson's questionable, superficial ability than to pull out of Jimmy what Jimmy knew he was capable of doing—'a piece of work comparable to Clift's in that movie.'

"Jimmy felt he was being sacrificed for Rock Hudson—and for Taylor—he wasn't pleased about it—he was burning. He said, 'Hudson doesn't like me—shit, what am I saying, the guy *hates* me!' Jimmy and Stevens weren't getting along very well about that issue either, and that was a gross understatement.

"'Dammit,' he said, 'I know I'm a much better actor than what's being done with me at the moment.' He said, 'I'm being inhibited—restricted, I'm not able to exercise the capacity of my abilities.'"

After Jimmy left the bike in Santa Monica that day, he had me ride him around and around some section of the area until we'd found a huge storm drain.

We rode down into it, running the bike up and down along the concrete embankment wall—a lot of fun; through the water in the bottom of the bed and up and down the sides, laughing our asses off.

We stopped and sat on the steep concrete and smoked a reefer as an old inner tube sort of wiggled along in the water. Jimmy said when he was eight or so years old he'd tried to make a flower box for his mom. The kind with a metal hinge on the front that could be opened so the pots could be taken out.

"I couldn't get it screwed to the bottom the right way," he said. "Had to have a small piano hinge, you know? I wanted my father to help.... He never did. I threw the box away."

He said he wondered what happens to things like that, when they get lost—are they still stored in the brain? He imagined the idea of the brain as a sort of radio. "That we tune in to things," he said. "And if it isn't still in the brain, would it be in the air?"

I said I thought things would be in the air.

"Everything that's lived and everything that's died," he said, "may be floating past us right now."

Maybe, I said. We laughed. Stoned.

"So everything's waves—air waves," he said. "Your brain can be naked and you can turn the radio dial and get everything that's in the air, everything that's been lost."

"But it doesn't come back," I said. "You can only hear it like a mystery show—" We kept laughing.

After he got the newer, big-bore engine, we rode to Sammy Davis, Jr.'s, and parked the bikes by his house. Sammy wanted to go for a spin. Jimmy took off with Sammy on the back— around the hills, taking the corners fast—leaning, and then raced really fast coming back up, but he was blowing a lot of smoke.

Sammy climbed off the bike wobbling but grinning like he was stoned. "Wow!" he said. "Wow, man, what a fucking *gas!*"

He insisted we stay for lunch and his grandmother opened cans of broth, cut up vegetables, and threw a hunk of ham in the pot. Sammy poured some fancy wine Dean Martin had given him, and after stuffing our faces, Sammy didn't want us to leave.

"You guys have to *stay*, man. This is Sunday, isn't it? Who cares what day it is! We've got to have a party—we got to get loaded and have an orgy—" He quickly said, "I got a phone book of the hottest chicks in town, man. All you got to do is run your finger through the book like you do in a yellow pages."

Sammy wanted him to stay, and whenever he looked at Jimmy, his face seemed to explode into bursts of light. So the afternoon changed into another bongo-drum party with Jimmy getting stoned and beating the skins. Sammy danced and shook mmaracas at his hi-fi speakers while other people seemed to arrive out of nowhere, thickening the group like chunks of starch in his grandmother's soup.

Sammy kept bouncing and throwing his arms around Jimmy. "This is the cat I *love!*" he'd announce to everybody. "The one that I *love!*"

Still stoned the next day, Jimmy said he'd had a flash—an idea, "a joke," he said, and giggled about it. We'd get a super-charged hot rod and play ting-a-ling. Only I'd be dressed up as a chick, with a big blonde wig and red high heels. I'd have "lot of makeup like a French whore—like a black mask."

He said we'd go a hundred miles an hour in a trail like a snake, making bumpers ring all the way across town from the ocean to the desert.

"What [was] frightening," Eartha says, "was people were saying Jimmy's running around on these motorcycles and he's going to kill himself.

"Other people have said to me he's wanting to kill himself, it's what he's after with racing those cars, why he's doing it, but funny... I never thought so at first.

"He gave off a feeling that is inexplicable," she says. "His popularity went deep into you. That is what's frightening....

"The person he was looking for within himself, I think he liked, though he hadn't gotten to know that person. I think he really and truly did like himself; he was very curious and very keen to bring that person to the fore. He liked acting because within it he found all sorts of facades inside of himself and he was fascinated by them.

"But actually as far as being interested in the real value of James Dean, I have never found anybody around him that was that interested. Maybe they thought they were, but they never actually opened themselves up to get him to come out. If you want to know someone you have to open yourself up in order to bring that person in, to allow that person to exercise what he or she wants."

One night, Eartha recalls, "we were all at a get-together, meeting up with our friends and some of Jimmy's people arrived. He said, 'Oh, Kitt, come and get in the car with me—I want to go someplace and get some records.' And I got into this sports car with him, and he was driving around the

Hollywood Hills to get to wherever it was he was staying or where he had his things—I don't think he ever slept there.

"Suddenly we see someone following us in another sports car—a girl with him. Jimmy parked so he could fetch his records. I waited in the car for him. When he came out of the house, he got in the car and straightaway started to race like mad.

"The guy behind us started to race, too. All of a sudden there was this terrible noise behind us. We stopped and saw that the guy had run his car off the road and up the side of the mountain. There was a small fire. He and the girl got out, and we went back to inspect—to see if they were hurt. The fellow, who was a photographer, was brushing himself off, laughing and joking, and Jimmy said, 'You can't do the things I'm doing. I can flirt with death and come through—you can't.'"

That was when Eartha began to fear for Jimmy, She believed that what he'd said showed a "dangerous streak" that was rising to the surface.

"He didn't seem concerned about what had happened," she says, "or that someone—anyone, might've gotten killed just as easily as not.

"Going back, I said to him, 'I don't like this car or these motorcycles. One of these cars is going to kill you.' He laughed and told me to stop it, to quit talking like that and play drums and dance at the party instead."

At that party, Eartha encouraged Jimmy into a sort of modern African dance to the music and drums. Jimmy'd put on a long sort of cannibal-looking mask with big teeth sticking out of it, and Eartha donned the chalk-white Japanese Kabuki mask of a girl—tiny red lips and black eyes, and hair as black as a raven's wing.

Before the filming of *Rebel* was completed, Jimmy visited my mother, who'd been under a movie contract in the thirties, in

Hollywood. He told her about his own mother, about her dying when he was nine and about how he didn't think he'd been close to anyone since then, "not in the sense of being able to be a part of someone," he said. Jimmy asked her a number of personal and penetrating questions having to do with her own inability to provide a home for me during most of my life. He wanted to know how that affected her feelings for me, and if she'd felt that I had been able to come to terms with feelings of my own, how that could have caused some lack of affection between mother and son.

On one of his visits, I sketched a picture of him on canvas with a skull in the background, like in the photo with Dennis Hopper. When he looked at it, he said, "Make the skull laughing." I said okay and tried, but it never came off. I could never envision a skull laughing; I couldn't figure out how it would work. Finally I just scrubbed out the lower jaw. The next time he saw it, it was Jimmy who was laughing.

"That's him," he said, "the old fuck—the one who's been riding my butt…. Look at the son of a bitch—he's got nothing in his eye sockets."

The young German mechanic for Porsche cars, Rolf Wutherich, met Jimmy at a sports car-race in Bakersfield. Jimmy was racing his Speedster.

"I was looking over the Porsche cars," Rolf says, "and got to talking with Jimmy, who won that race as well as a couple of others near Santa Barbara. He lacked experience—took unsafe chances, but I felt he had that essential feel for fast cars. I thought he showed that he had that sixth sense a racing driver can't do without."

Two weeks later, Rolf met with Jimmy in Hollywood. "He had a small rubber monkey that he kept bouncing up and down on a rubber band," Rolf says. "'I got to talk to you,' Jimmy said to me." He wanted to enter the big-car class in his

next race. This was the class for cars with larger, more powerful engines, taking place in an airstrip race three hundred
miles north of Los Angeles on the first of October.

Jimmy said, "I want to be on top." He told Rolf he was getting a Bristol racer from an English dealer, and Rolf then
remembered the Porsche Spyder that was on sale at
Competition Motors.

"This was a very special machine, a rare car," Rolf says. "I
told Jimmy he would have to see it, have to get the feel of it
since he was already driving Porsches. The Spyder, I said,
might be just what he needed to make his dream come true."

The next day Jimmy was at Competition Motors to look
over the Spyder. He drove it around the block only once and
said he'd buy it. "It's like taking ahold of a thunderbolt,"
Jimmy said. But before he made arrangements to pay for the
car, he asked Rolf to agree to a condition: that the mechanic
would personally check the car and go over it before each race
that Jimmy planned to enter, and that Rolf would ride with
him to the first race as the car's mechanic. The filming of
Giant was scheduled to end shortly before that, and since
Jimmy's contract didn't allow him to drive in races until the
completion of the picture, he'd have to wait until the last
minute before taking part in the race.

That was a problem, Rolf said. "Before entering such a
race," Rolf says he told Jimmy, "a driver should have time to
get acquainted with the car. The Spyder should be driven at
least five hundred miles by the driver entering in the competition....

"Jimmy was too eager," Rolf says, but suggested a last-
minute compromise. They would drive the car, not haul the
Spyder by trailer to the race. "That way, "Rolf says, "Jimmy
would drive it up there instead, and get the feel of the car."

Jimmy and Rolf agreed that was the only way to do it. "But
there remained a doubt in my mind," Rolf says, "an uncertainty

In Texas with Elizabeth Taylor during the making of *Giant*, "Some fine, fine, gorgeous lady is Liz..."

that stayed with me that Jimmy might not have familiarized himself enough with the car to race it with confidence once we got on the track."

Quite some time before Warner Brothers laid down the law against Jimmy engaging in racing while making a picture, George Stevens was privately seeking some key to unlock

219

Jimmy's resistance. "We're at loggerheads," Stevens said.

Several confrontations over conflicting interpretations now prompted Stevens to chase some resolution before the production suffered more than it already had. Dean's plain "unmanageableness," his tardiness, "his souring resistance to reasonable demands differing from what *he* has in mind" was "depleting the entire company."

"Who in the hell does he think he *is*?" Stevens roared. "This is a *George Stevens* production—this is not a James *Dean* production!"

The problems were viewed as erupting from "a kind of germ in Dean," and the front office was asking; Could the disharmony get so bad as to cause the studio to lose money?

Elbers said the answer was yes, and quickly offered a possible way to examine everyone's concerns—including Dean's.

"We need a mediator," he said. "Someone basically who Dean feels he might trust—perhaps a Texan with some special understanding of the people in question. We hire this person in on a one-shot technical consultation," to discuss interpretations of the characters in the script, "get a feel for what he's after—for what's the matter with Dean."

At the same time, Elbers suggested, the mediator could equally serve the success of the production by sharing with Stevens whatever insights he gathers related to managing Dean…"something that may strike harmony for the sake of the picture and avoid any further problems."

However, Emory Miller, the "technical consultant" met Jimmy with a somewhat altered agenda. A skilled, professional psychologist, Miller embarked on his interview with Dean focusing on Jimmy and not on Dean's problems with portraying a character in the movie.

At the same time, Miller skillfully steered the consultation through the conflicts of the fictional character, using Jett Rink as his pivotal point for getting into Dean's head.

Jimmy would've scoffed at the idea of consulting a shrink. He'd entertained seeing Brando's only to gain more of an identification with Brando—same as he'd wanted with Clift. He'd learned from Donna Reed that Clift drove with an enraged, frenzied foot on the gas. He loved speed—thrilling to the blast of an engine and sound of the tires screaming.

"Everybody had to get out of Monty's way," said Reed. "He'd blow the horn—swerve this way and that, and he'd actually pull into the oncoming lane of traffic on a busy street to get around someone going too slow for Monty. And he passed cars on the right," Reed said, "what they call the 'suicide' side."

Jimmy had a wad of theories he wanted to discuss with Miller. He said, "I can't get them across to Mr. Stevens. He just won't listen to me, but I can't work in this picture if he's trying to stop me from doing it."

Unlike Kazan who had a way of reaching inside his actors, working through them, Stevens gathered around him the cast and crew in order to get them to work through Stevens—the goal being to create on film the picture Stevens has carried in his mind, peculiar to Stevens.

"As Jimmy accuses me of interfering with his work, I can only say that I feel he is jeopardizing *my* work. And I am the one running the show...not Dean."

17.

Dying is Easy

E artha Kitt was in New York with a play, and returned
to Hollywood that summer in 1955 for a recording session. A couple of days later she went to a mutual
friend's house, and Jimmy opened the door. She was surprised
to see him.

"He hugged me and kissed me as he always did," she says,
"and I hugged him back, but I couldn't feel him.... It was the
strangest sensation. I said, 'What's the matter with you? I
don't feel you.' And he said, 'Kitt, you're being a witch again,
baby. Be *real*."

He had to talk to her. It was urgent, he said. He told her
he'd been able to confide in someone, "a consultant who *lis-
tens*," he said. "Maybe I can get through to this fucking
Stevens with this guy as a pipeline."

Eartha realized this conversation was simply a continuation
of their last. "He didn't ask about my play or what I was doing
back in town." Everything that had gone wrong, he said, was

to be blamed on the director's stubbornness and "Hitler-like control of the cast...

"I knew what Jimmy was saying," Eartha says. "We sat for a while holding hands and he kept squeezing my hand nervously. He looked strange and nervous and jittery, and like he'd jump when he heard some sound.

The picture was going too big in an artificial way, he told her that day. "Jimmy wanted it to be more artistic. He wanted the interpretation of him as an old man to be quite different from what it was turning out to be.

"He said he didn't even want to see the picture. He said, 'That's not me, that's not where I want to go.' He said Stevens didn't help him mature the character in the way the character should have matured and grown to be at the end of the picture.

"The problems he was having with *Giant*, that sort of frustration, is real heavy to carry. How to handle an individual, that's what Hollywood is all about. If you're run-of-the-mill, if you can sing so that the housewives think they can sing in the bathtub as well as you can, then you're in. Or if you look just about the average face, then 'okay.' But if you're very beautiful or if you're looking for that individual inside of yourself in order to act at all, if you're very different—then there's frustration.

"What they needed was a stuffed doll. I think that's all that Hollywood can handle."

What had worked so beautifully in *East of Eden* under the artful direction of Elia Kazan was now a crashing B-29 for Jimmy. Novelist Edna Ferber was viewing the rushes and said, "James Dean is a genius." But success, she felt, was poisoning him.

"He wanted to run away," Eartha said, "but he couldn't.

Sometimes it's best to lie dormant for a while. You have to wait for all the trash to get out of the way."

Dennis Hopper who'd worked in *Rebel*, was playing Rock Hudson's son in *Giant*. When *Rebel* was finished, Jimmy was "sitting on the top of the world," says Dennis. "Like Cagney in *White Heat*—'Hey, mom! Top of the world!'

"He'd *made* it, man," says Dennis. "And then Stevens came along to deliberately pull it out from under Dean. Jimmy entered *Giant* only to meet head-on with all that he'd said he hated and probably feared—resistance to his sense of and need for control.

"Stevens demanded that Dean take a sideline seat, as if he had nothing to do in the film except to play background to Rock Hudson and Elizabeth Taylor, whose performances, Jimmy felt, were so superficial, so poor, sodden.... And he was *expected* to take it seriously. It was demanded of him that he take it seriously.

"He couldn't, and yet what he did do in the picture is so incredible. His performance stands out as the high point of Stevens' extravaganza.

"I mean it was a deliberate thing. I don't know why Stevens had it in for him so much, except that Jimmy seemed to intimidate the man, to cast a bad light on Stevens while they were working because he rebuffed Stevens, he didn't agree with everything Stevens wanted to do.

"Stevens wasn't interested in whether you agreed with him or not. It was the law, man. The Ten Commandments: 'Thou shalt honor, obey, and respect the director.'"

There was nothing to negotiate.

"I was *there*," says Dennis. "I know Stevens was rude to Dean and brushed him aside. So Jimmy started to booze a lot and he'd be late and he'd be sarcastic and he just started fucking off. Okay, so he was getting even."

It was apparent to Dennis that Stevens wasn't going to try to bring Jimmy over to his side. "No, he just kept sticking up that sign that says, 'I'm Stevens and this is a Stevens big-money picture and everybody's gotta bow and scrape and grovel over here.' He'd sometimes treated Dean like a fool—a stupid jackoff. He berated him in front of the crew and cast, in front of a lot of people to humiliate him.

"And all these people came from all over to see Jimmy Dean; they were all over Texas looking for him and bugging people on the set. This is what got to Stevens. It was as if Jimmy was the only thing happening."

But Jimmy's misery pressed inward into him as sharp as the points on a child's jack—as deep as the arrows in Saint Sebastian.

Liz Taylor moved from the sidelines, attracted to Jimmy's misery. At least for that short period of time on location in Texas, Jimmy found in Liz, another "soul mate," another pair of cradling arms.

An ex-filmloader, now in Colorado, recalls that Texas location as a "hot spot, so hot you'd blister your butt sitting in your trailer."

Taylor's friendship with Jimmy during that time has been described by various writers as a platonic relationship with Jimmy while making *Giant*, and erroneously lumping Jimmy with other "homosexual male actors" Taylor was friendly with, including Clift.

The filmloader says he saw "them kissing one night between two trailers. Her tongue was practically into his throat.

"I had availability to the locations the three stars were situated in, and Taylor was several times in Jimmy's location until the very early hours of the morning.

Rock Hudson intensely disliked Dean, but claimed the "intense friendship they developed in Marfa" was an extension of how most of the actors felt—"like we were in cages." He says, "Dean was a very depressed person and Liz took to him in a most motherly fashion. Whether she was in and out of his bed or he was in and out of her bed or whether no one was in anyone's bed is really no one's business but their own."

Elber says, "We needed to find the chink in Dean's armor to get him to do what we wanted him to do. We couldn't fire him—couldn't suspend him: he was the hottest actor in town."

What was his problem—why couldn't he cooperate?

Meanwhile, complicating the issue, was Karen Davis and her pregnancy.

"Pay her off and send her away," was the word from the front office.

Dr. Miller had spent the best part of a morning listening to an unsuspecting Jimmy funnel his turmoils into the psychologist's ear.

"First off," Miller said, "Dean *has* to be great—he has to see himself as a great personality, having some great achievement. Or he sees himself as a failure.

"Things seem in the extreme—he's either great, has to be great, or he's crumpled and a failure. He thinks he is failing in this film, is failing to bring to the surface what he experienced in the first movie he made, and to a somewhat lesser degree, the second one as well.

"He won't buy the hit-and-miss idea most everyone understands, the 'you can't win them all' theory. Dean has to win them all or he's throwing in the towel.

"I tried to tell him that he hit pay dirt with the Kazan movie, that was a positive fluke, and he cannot possibly measure a future against a past success that was, after all, not totally in his control."

Elbers made it clear that Dr. Miller wasn't Jimmy's psychologist. He was a consultant—and as such had reserved no obligation of confidentiality.

Miller said, "What seems a narcissistic personality is just

that in this instance. Dean shows a remarkable—if well-intoned at times—sense of exaggerated self-exhibition. He seeks constant admiration, constant attention, and it has to be the kind of attention he's after, not what you're particularly willing to give. That's the crux of his present difficulties.... He is a young man who is starving, who wants only Roman Meal bread. He won't eat the Langendorf bread. So he'll starve to death unless he is forced to eat."

Miller said Dean perceived the present situation as a definite threat to his self-esteem. "He's exploitive and manipulative. He's very clever and has a definite, exaggerated sense of self-importance and self-absorption.

"As an accomplished actor, he no doubt has exceptional ability. The only things holding him back are the threats to his self-esteem, and the restrictions placed on him by others.

"Certainly this is the medium we're in—but Dean is convinced inside of himself that the work should be an open arena for James Dean to shine in whatever fashion he seizes upon."

The psychologist surmised that Dean had a "personality disorder... he responds to any criticism in a manner of defeat. Criticism reduces him to feelings of inferiority, feeling of being emptied of substance.

"He has rage in him, and he will rage against these criticisms and restrictions in a number of ways. Curiously," said Miller, "I find contradictions here—his identification with the Jett Rink character as an outgrowth of himself; the pining away for a lost love—some unrequited love that literally runs him ragged psychologically. Well, I think Dean suffers from some of this himself and wastes away internally.

"He doesn't have the ability to conquer outright, to seize or take a woman as he must, or put himself in the character's boots and seize the woman. He won't—he mopes, he pines, and becomes emptied, and this is the crux with Mr. Stevens—

he doesn't want him moping and pining, but Dean wants to mope and cry. This is what he knows best—what has brought him the most attention and admiration.

"The problem as I see it," said Miller, "is that Jimmy Dean has bit off more than he can chew, and it's a problem he's trying to face repeatedly, with ever-increasing wear and tear psychologically. Whenever he is required to act a part that is not a direct extension of himself, and he knows this, he will be convinced he is failing—that it's all a disaster.

"He can shake his fists against the sky, but he is only raging at the wind."

Miller suggested that Jimmy could not be swayed from the preoccupation with himself. "The difficulties as I see them," he said, "cannot be resolved."

All that Stevens could do, Miller advised, was perhaps direct attention to the character. "To feed into the motivation behind Dean's narcissism," he said. "When he does something, praise him loudly—let him take the credit for whatever it is. Let Dean think he is the real hot dog.

"He's not going to try to please you or anyone. Give him as much creative license as you can and don't have expectations of his doing something the way you want it done.

He will have to do it his way, in order to be successful."

But Stevens said no. No. A resounding *"No!"* He said, "The day I'm forced to be subservient to an actor's whims is the day they can plant me in the daisies."

Fourteen days after the actual filming of *Giant* was completed, shortly before eight on the last morning of September, Jimmy showed up at Competition Motors eager to get the Spyder on the road.

Rolf finished his coffee while he checked the Porsche engine, the oil, ignition, spark plugs, and tires. Jimmy walked back and forth, watching him, suggesting he was taking too

Trying "the feel" of a British race car during the last meet Jimmy entered.

long and could he help to speed things up?

"You'll only complicate it," Rolf told him. Jimmy sat and leafed through newspapers and old magazines. One of the last things Rolf did was to fix a safety belt for the driver. There was no need for one on the passenger's seat, as Jimmy would be racing alone. Finally Jimmy got in the car and pulled the belt on. It snapped shut.

It was a few minutes after ten when Sandy Roth and actor

Bill Hickman showed up, ready for the drive north in Jimmy's station wagon with the flat trailer hitched. Jimmy started the engine.

For months Rolf would lay in the hospital in casts "with my face lost in weird wire structures" because of his shattered jaw. He'd undergo a bone-grafting operation to reconnect his hipbone with an eight-inch silver nail and screws. "While I lay there," Rolf says, "I looked and looked into my memory to recall those few seconds before the accident."

Warners was paying Rolf's bills, working out a settlement. "We had to batten down all hatches," Rosen says, "and close off all the leaks that could've hurt us at the box office. Tell a clean story.

"But these problems—immediate as they were—paled against the advantages to be realized from Dean's movies. Everyone who didn't like him suddenly loved him. Getting his image on a positive course and keeping it going until we'd squeezed every nickle out of these pictures.

"The front office was furious. With the crocodile tears, Dean was detested—hated for dying just as he'd climbed the hill of fame. He'd cheated us—he cheated everybody. No one, but no one, except some prophet could've predicted the extent of the industry's profits generated by the James Dean image. No one. With his face decades later on a postage stamp, he's got to be up there somewhere laughing his ass off at us."

"Was there an instant before he died," asked Rolf, "when he knew that he was dying? That was what I wanted to know. Did he do it as a test—as a test of himself to see if he could do it? Did he know that death was what he was chasing?"

Grabbing a smoke at sports car races; running the Speedster "Flat out—all the way to win."

18.

Fork in the Road

The sky was white, almost burning. Highway 466 was deserted, two lanes winding westward—a long, downgrade stretch. No other car except the Spyder. With the station wagon far behind on the desolate stretch, Jimmy pushed on the gas.

Low in the afternoon sky, the sun was shining directly into their eyes. Rolf adjusted his sunglasses and watched the heat flicker and dance on the black road. On all sides the land rolled in yellow hills.

"Everything is okay," Rolf said. "It is best if you ease up a little."

At moments the horizon seemed long and stretched out. More hills under a sea of short weeds. The Spyder engine was steady and high-pitched. It was singing. Jimmy had both hands on the wheel and was staring straight ahead. He said the land reminded him a lot of Indiana—only it was darker there, the earth was darker, and the sun was never so bright.

Rolf glanced at him, then returned his eyes to the road. They climbed a hill and rounded a gradual bend in the road, then were heading straight on a long length of highway. Way up ahead was a tiny speck, a dark spot on the road like a kind of pencil point shimmering as it grew larger, almost imperceptibly.

"Cholame..." Jimmy was saying, pointing one gloved hand in the direction they were heading. "Nothing there but a post office—it's a shed, man," he said. The tiny hamlet of Cholame—just a stop in the road a short distance past the fork where Highway 41 branched off 466. That tiny black spot they'd seen in the road was another car heading east— approaching from the opposite lane.

"The vibration of the road and speed seemed to cause a sort of haze in front of us," Rolf says. "I leaned a little bit to the left to look around the glass. Jimmy was burning too much on the downgrade—it was unnecessary; he didn't understand the car. At the speed we were traveling, the distance between the Spyder and that other car, apparently slowing down, was shortened with incredible swiftness. It looked to me like the other car was stopping in the intersection at that turnoff and waiting for us to come ahead and pass before he made his left turn onto 41."

Suddenly the other car seemed to swerve or jerk forward over the center line directly into the path of the Spyder.

"Motherfucker!" Jimmy said. "What the heck is he doing?"

Jimmy hit the brakes and the shriek of rubber burning on the asphalt was a short, piercing noise.

"All I saw was that car—big—black and white, leaping in front of us like a wall that suddenly cuts right in your path and I was sliding into the ground....

"We'd already hit the car before I was sure we had or what had happened, but we were glancing off to the side. The noise of the impact and collision was deafening and it kept echoing, even though it had all happened in fractions of a second, and

I had the horrible feeling of having no control over my body. My head struck something and I was then outside of the car on the ground—on the dirt of the roadside."

Everything was dark—the sky had disappeared. Then it turned to red, "and then it was light," Rolf says, "but I couldn't move my body and I didn't know what kind of a position my body was in. There was a loud hissing and the air was all dust. Metal seemed to be creaking and I thought, 'My god—we've had an accident!' That's what was in my thoughts. We'd been in a bad accident."

Rolf tried raising his head. Someone was running. He could later remember the sound of someone's feet on the road. The noise of metal cracking had stopped but there was still some hissing or a high-pitched whining noise in Rolf's ears. He couldn't move his mouth. He raised his right hand a little and brought it up to feel his face but saw there wasn't any skin on his hand.

"It looked like a piece of hamburger before you cook it, and blood was spurting out of all the tiny red spots in the flesh. I could taste blood in my mouth and someone was saying, 'Oh, Jesus! Oh, Jesus!' but I couldn't move any other part of my body. I couldn't feel my hand and I couldn't see anything except that patch of dirt where my face was."

Only later would Rolf learn what had happened while he had dropped into and out of unconsciousness.

The Porsche had smashed into the other car, spun around, and crashed off the road in the ditch. Rolf came to momentarily as two men were lifting him on a stretcher into an ambulance.

"I could see the car. It looked like a tin-foil toy that had been stepped on, and I could see Jimmy—still in the car. His arms were outstretched to the sides as it looked to me from that angle, and his head was tipped sideways as if he was looking to the side and up into the air. As if someone had said, 'Look, see what is flying there!'

Highway 466. Last photo taken of Jimmy (alive), only a few miles to the crash at Cholame.

"I was seeing things as if through a smoke screen, a terrible haze, but someone was saying that we had to leave him in the car until the coroner could get to where we were."

The station wagon had jammed to a stop and Sandy Roth with Bill Hickman came running to the wrecked car.

Bill said that Jimmy was dead.

Rolf says, "Someone stepped in front of the car and put a blanket over the seat section of the Spyder. Jimmy's form beneath the blanket appeared like a ghost with the arms reaching out to the sides."

Then everything went black.

.   .   .

The Spyder being towed from the fatal accident site, September 30, 1955.

Karen remembers sitting cross-legged in yellow pajamas that September 30, 1955, late at night, listening to the Chordettes singing "Mister Sandman" when news of "the tragic death of meteoric movie star James Dean" interrupted the music.

She'd been sorting photographs for a new composite— intending to use the shots Jimmy had taken. She hadn't heard anything about him in more than two weeks. She wasn't even sure whether *Giant* was finished or if they were still shooting.

Her first thought was that she hadn't heard right. Next, that the news was some kind of weird joke. It had to be—she'd actually been thinking about Jimmy seconds before the interruption, and all because of the photo of her which he'd said made her face look square and a bit like a blonde Ann Blyth "playing Goldilocks," he'd said. And then the disc jockey said he was dead and Karen hadn't finished that thought yet, hadn't even played it out.

"I tried to hide myself under the bathroom sink," she says, "but that was no place to hide. If he was really dead—when had he died? Would some part of him still be in the air—in space somehow, and could I connect to it if I killed myself right away? The question of how to do it, how to kill myself quickly. I didn't have a gun. I couldn't cut my own throat. I could hang myself, though, and I started thinking of what I could use to hang myself and where I could tie up the thing so I could hang there and what would work for that purpose.... But I kept thinking about Modigliani, the painter. Jimmy and I'd talked about him and his dying so young, and then his mistress—the girl that was pregnant with Modigliani's baby—ran and threw herself out of a window, killing herself and the baby in her womb."

Karen saw the red phone cord lying across the floor tiles and she pulled on it until she had the receiver in her hands. She shakily dialed Billy Gunn's number, and as soon as he answered, she screamed into the phone, "He's dead! He's dead—"

"I know he's dead," Billy said.

Someone called me down in the Village but by then I was already on my way uptown. They talked to Hugh, a writer friend I was staying with, and they said they were afraid Karen would "take those pills she'd got....What's going on? Is Dean really dead or not?—I mean, how can Jimmy Dean be dead?"

About forty minutes before that I was sitting on the couch in Hugh's living room, screwing around with a story I was writing when the news broke, and Hugh was suddenly standing in the door, white, weird-looking skinny shoulders sticking out of his lost hipster's undershirt, a beard crumpling his cheeks, bread caught in its shoebrush about the jaw.

He spoke very slowly: "Did they just say he was killed?"

We stayed there stiff, stunned for moments, wanting to hear

the rest of it, some kind of explanation…but there wasn't any more to hear, it was over and the music had taken up the beat from where it had been interrupted. "You better go see Karen," murmured Hugh.

It seemed that I should take something with me. I stuffed matches into my shirt pocket. Shocked, but feeling as if I were a kid and sort of riding on the crest of a wave that was maybe coming to beach in Santa Monica—an odd feeling, like I should throw up my arms, make a proclamation.

If I tried hard I could still feel the cool ocean wind from that last motorcycle ride along Pacific Coast Highway, that last ride with Jimmy. We'd stopped at a cove cafe called La Mere and I'd said, "I'm freezing my ass off," and he'd unzipped the black cycle jacket he was wearing, pulled it off, and, leaning across his Triumph, handed it to me. "You wear this if you want it." He only had a T-shirt on.

I said, "You'll freeze."

He grinned and said, "I can't freeze, man, I'm a superstar!"

It occurred to me heading uptown on the subway that I'd have to see the body to be convinced he was dead. Death had been the joke, not a joke that you laugh at "ha ha" but something that is understood should not be taken at face value. Death meant something else: it stood for a way of seeing the world around us. Leave it to the phonies to point out the signs of a death wish, or comment on how self-destructive we were—signs that were supposed to be flying rampant.

On the subway I looked around at the people and wondered who else knew he'd been killed, and what would it mean to them. Did they know what they'd lost? Did they understand?

I didn't understand it myself.

In Karen's bathroom, the door closed, I tried to get her to climb out from under the sink. A couple others were in the living room, waiting. It was like we were all supposed to get together and do something. I didn't know what it was.

Karen said, "Jonathan—" and she pressed the heels of her hands into her belly. "I'm pregnant with Jimmy's child." "So I've been told," I said.

"What should I do now?" she asked.

I didn't know. I finally talked her out of the bathroom, and she cried for a long time on the couch. The rest of us—there was the girlfriend of Johnny Saxon's and that guy from the theater, and Barry Shrode was there—watched Karen cry. Each of us felt it deeply but perhaps in different ways.

After it got light, Karen and I walked along Central Park South and then she stopped and looked at me. Her eyes were red. "He's gone," she said. "He's gone."

By morning she wasn't crying anymore.

Eartha Kitt says he took long walks in the twilight of the New York park. "Jamie was a good guy. Sometimes I feel very regretful about someone who can be born into a people who never really knew him. You can go to a priest and you can confess and think that priest knows you, you've emptied your soul out to that person. But they don't know you, not really. That's the most frustrating thing. You keep hoping they do, that they know your spirit as they know you as a body, and they can communicate with your spirit.... But we don't have the time to get into this—we're too busy doing our own thing.

"I'm richer from having known James Dean. He altered my life. I feel that he's never left it.

"He gave out electronic waves. Who could tune in to those waves? And then, too, there are so many lonely people—you can tune in on that. That's what his impact was. And many more tuned in on it than we can imagine.

"I saw *Giant* at the opening premiere in London. I sat and looked at the film and I found myself in an absolute state of aloneness.

"When the film was over, the feeling that I got from him, I didn't want to share with anyone or talk to anyone, I didn't want to see another person. I'd been escorted by Sidney Poitier, and we both got up and I just kept walking. I don't know what happened to Sidney.

"It was raining. I just kept walking. Piccadilly Circus. I lived several streets away from there, and I was all dressed up in an evening gown and a fur coat and diamonds, and the prostitutes were coming on to me because usually I stop and talk to these girls because there have been times I was walking to my hotel and these girls have protected me. But they couldn't touch me now. This was the night that I wasn't really there."

They had an oxygen mask over Jimmy's face as the ambulance hurried the fifteen miles to Paso Robles, even though they knew he was dead.

It was determined at the War Memorial Hospital in Paso Robles that Dean had died instantly. From there, his body had been delivered to a funeral home where it was processed for transportation to Indiana.

This time Jimmy's father Winton accompanied the coffin after it was arranged for Jimmy to be taken to Hunt Mortuary, in Fairmount.

The coffin was flown from Burbank Airport instead of Los Angeles International, to avoid publicity. It was night and Jimmy's father was alone, sending the body back to Indiana for burial as he'd once sent him as a child, along with the body of the boy's mother—his wife.

Mr. Hunt was waiting at the airport in Indiana to take delivery of the coffin. It was loaded into Hunt's hearse and Winton and Hunt drove to Fairmount in silence.

Jimmy was buried a week later on October 8 in Fairmount. Karen traveled from New York to attend his funeral and said she was surprised to see "quite a few of the crowd from Googie's." She said, "The Reverend said Jimmy's career hasn't ended. It's just beginning and God Himself is directing the production."

She took snapshots of the flowers and the wreaths, sent them to friends. Back in New York, her hands shook as she showed me more pictures. "Nobody ever saw Jimmy's body," she said. "There's rumors starting about him not really being dead. They're saying it was Rolf that got killed, not Jimmy, who's hospitalized someplace else." She started to cry.

She said, "Look at this," and pulled up her sweater. She took my hands and placed them against her body. "My tummy is swelling with the baby," she said.

"What are you going to do?" I asked.

"I'm going to my mom's—in Toronto. I'm going to have the baby there and then I'm going back to L.A."

Her dark eyes were moist—sort of far off looking, almost squinting. They made me think of Jimmy's eyes after we'd sat through *A Place in the Sun* for the third time. We'd left the movie theater and were walking to Forty-seventh and Eighth in the rain, stopping to look in empty windows and then walking on.

It was light still and I was wearing a mackinaw with holes in the sleeves and Jimmy had on an old black raincoat. By the time we got to Forty-seventh we were soaked. Rain kept pouring down over his forehead and down the bridge of his nose, dripping off his nose and chin. He laughed at me at the corner of Forty-seventh and Eighth, and I remember the way he looked at that moment—completely out of touch with his surroundings, yet at the same time such an integral part of them.

19.

Road's End

We were going to converge on Cholame and have a party at the place of Dean's death. A private affair we had trouble getting together. It'd been Nick Adams' idea. He'd envisioned a train of mourners trekking north through the fields of Bakersfield, snaking up Highway 99 to 466. Sal Mineo said he'd come. Dennis Hopper was supposed to be riding with Nick and bringing Seffi Sydney—a bit player from *Rebel*. Nick tried to get Natalie but she couldn't be reached. "Out of town or out of commission."

Liz Taylor later said she thought Dennis Hopper had told her about the party, and she thought it was "morbid and certainly tasteless."

Frank Mazzolla who'd appeared in *Rebel*, and had attended Hollywood High with me, said he was on his way to Cholame. A couple of guys with custom cars were supposed to show up. They didn't. A writer for a British magazine, Bruce Taylor, driving a rented blue Volkswagen, was taping the trip on a

Jimmy's coffin—burial in Fairmont, October 8, 1955.

battered reel-to-reel recorder, with Karen and myself as his passengers.

Jack Simmons was bringing up the rear in the hearse—a fitting, ironic touch. Jack and I hadn't said very much since the accident. I knew he'd broken into Jimmy's new place in Sherman Oaks the minute he heard he'd been killed. He'd loaded that same hearse with as much as he could carry out of Jimmy's—all personal stuff: photos, letters, clothes. He'd brought cardboard boxes, so I'd been told, and packed them as tight as he could. He'd filled the hearse and then hidden the stuff. In time to come, he'd keep the booty in a small, seemingly vacant storefront on Santa Monica Boulevard, with a painted-over window. It would remain there for a long time, until one weekend a leaking pipe between the stores would burst and flood both shops. The same sort of break-in had happened to Jimmy's small apartment in New York following the news of his death. Vampira'd declined the Cholame trip but Jack had two other Googie customers in tow, one with a case of Lucky Lager.

243

Karen wasn't drinking because she was now five months pregnant, but actually looked just fat in a long, sloppy, black raincoat. I was drinking in the backseat and already into a second quart of Ballentine.

Nick Adams was driving a powder blue Chevy station wagon, and laughing and fooling around with a few kids he'd brought—one from some Idaho college and the other a kind of albino. The girl in the middle seat was Sue, small head, cute face, a little like a yellow-headed chipmunk. She told me she was dating Dennis Hopper, and he'd said she might move in with him, "just for a little while," he'd said.

Few of us talked about Jimmy anymore. We did things about him in the sense that he was part of our actions, but we said very little about him. We were still "Jimmy's people."

Chuck Berry was on the VW radio as we rolled west along the last leg of the journey, into Blackwell's Corner parking lot, described by Bruce as a "gigantic area of wasted land surrounding a run-down building."

Earlier we'd all stopped at Tip's on the Grapevine for breakfast where Bruce continued taping his report on "James Dean's Last Day."

"Jimmy threw his jacket behind the seat of the low racing car," Bruce had said, "as they started the fateful trip north. " He'd guessed that Jimmy clipped his sun lenses over his regular glasses, and that traffic had been heavy leaving Hollywood.

With Rolf in the passenger's seat, the two drove out to Ventura Boulevard, filled the gas tank and reached Highway 99, cutting through the mountains between Los Angeles and Bakersfield.

"Sometimes Jimmy was leading," Bruce had said from what he'd learned from Bill Hickman, and "sometimes the station-wagon car with Bill and Sandy Roth in the lead."

Rolf kept lighting cigarettes for Jimmy because he didn't want Jimmy to get distracted or take his eyes off the road. Rolf would light the cigarettes hunching low under the windshield because the wind could tear the glowing tip of the cigarette away with it.

"The setting was ideal," Bruce recorded. "A fast, open race car on a sunny day with a long stretch of road ahead of them."

A few minutes before three in the afternoon they stopped at a roadside snack bar, ordered a glass of milk and a cup of coffee. Rolf drank coffee and ate a hot dog. He couldn't eat all of it, and Jimmy finished it off.

Rolf was feeling uneasy about the race in Salinas. He felt he'd better warn Jimmy: "Don't go too fast! Don't try to win! The Spyder is something quite different from the Speedster. Don't drive to win this one—drive only to get experience!"

Though Jimmy agreed, Rolf didn't believe that he wouldn't drive to win.

Bill and Sandy Roth pulled up in the station wagon and Sandy said, "You're driving way ahead of us. Don't let Jimmy drive too fast."

Jimmy climbed behind the wheel again and sped off onto the highway. But after a few minutes of driving, a Highway Patrol car pulled up close behind. After they stopped, the officer scribbled out a ticket for speeding. He'd said, "Way over the fifty-miles-per-hour limit."

The highway patrolman handed another summons to the driver of the station wagon. "The funny thing," Rolf said later, "was that the officer seemed to be more interested in the Porsche than in his summons, and Jimmy answered all his questions as if they were two drivers gabbing over a cup of coffee."

Before taking off again, Jimmy told Sandy and Bill that they'd meet at Paso Robles, have dinner there before heading north.

"Late afternoon by then," Bruce recorded, "the road was a thin dark line cutting through the monotonous landscape—

here and there a very slight bend, otherwise straight ahead. It must have been like driving that small white machine along the sharp edge of an endless ruler....

"The only break in the monotony was at Blackwell's Corner—a service station with a small store attached to it right in the middle of nowhere.

"When the station wagon caught up with Jimmy and his mechanic," Bruce went on, "Jimmy told his friends he planned on keeping the Porsche—which he said was his baby, for a long time to come." He then floored the accelerator and sped west on Highway 466—Blackwell's Corner having been his last stop.

Some didn't want to stop—they wanted to keep going, eager to get to the intersection of 41.

Nick bought more beer at Blackwells and everyone stood outside in a sun that was hot for November. It had a kind of blistering heat that seemed to penetrate your skin. One kid out of Jack Simmons' hearse had his hair bleached and combed like Jimmy's. He even had clip-on sunglasses.

Then we were on the road again, Nick roaring out ahead, his passengers bobbing in the car like corks. Karen said she was getting carsick and she shouldn't have made the trip. She thought of staying at Blackwell's—we'd pick her up on the way back. But no, Jack talked her into coming. He said he wouldn't have come if she'd planned to not go through with it.

She sort of lay halfway down on the backseat of the VW, and I rode in front with Bruce driving. The air was cold but the sun was hot. Karen asked me to roll the window up. She said she couldn't breathe.

"Please don't puke in the fucking car," Bruce said.

"I'm not going to puke," she said. The day before, I'd asked her if she was sure she was up to the long drive. She said she was. Every time our eyes met it was clear something had to be said to one another—something we had to understand. Maybe

Photos, letters, memorabilia of another time.

by joining in Nick Adams' stupid party trip to honor Jimmy, we'd somehow stumble into what it was we needed to say to one another.

She'd said, "I'd given thought to having a miscarriage before he was killed. Maybe it was the only way we could have been together—Jimmy and myself. We'd have to have done it without my being pregnant."

After Jimmy was dead, Stewart and I did a lot of talking, but the shadows stayed.

.   .   .

I didn't tell her he wouldn't have been with her anyway—pregnant or not. At first he'd thought it was maybe his kid, but the studio'd talked him out of it.

They had someone go to Marfa and talk to him—give him the story about Charlie Chaplin's parentage rap and the accused rape charge leveled at Errol Flynn years before. Jimmy'd said, "Well, if she isn't pregnant by me, then I don't want to be bothered with it."

He was told the possibility existed that she'd make some trouble, and Jimmy'd said to handle it any way they thought would get "the thing" taken care of. He said, "I can't be bothered with this sort of bullshit. If it isn't my kid, then why are you even talking to me about it? I don't know that I even fucked her, man. This is the chick that gave me a blowjob. How the hell's she supposed to get pregnant from giving me a blowjob?"

That was enough for the studio.

Yet he'd told me he'd fucked her. She was tight, he said, really tight. He'd had to push hard to get all the way in her.

Ever since breakfast at the Grapevine, I'd been telling myself the party trip was a big mistake. Half the people on it felt the same way the closer we got to that hill and then dreaded the thought of going over the hill. From that point you see straight down to Cholame. You could see that intersection.

Nick was driving as fast as he could to get there first. He'd said he knew pieces of the car were there. "You'll have to look around—they're there, in the roadside." He wanted to find pieces of the car.

I'd felt sick all morning.

Bruce the Britisher had expected a lot more out of me than I'd been giving him. He was hauling Karen back and forth in Hollywood. Shortly before, he'd almost talked her into going back to England with him to have "James Dean's baby" in London. If it was James Dean's baby. And now that Dean was dead, the plan was starting to stagnate.

I'd never have gone to Cholame on my own.

But there I was.

The cars were stopped across the highway. Nick's crew was pacing the intersection—tracking through the shoulder of the road. Nick had a drawing—a kind of map of exactly where the collision had occurred and where the Porsche had wound up. Sue was still in his car, perched and screwing lipstick over her mouth.

"You want some help getting out?" I asked Karen.

She shook her head.

"So here we are," she said. "Fucking windy here."

"And hot as shit," Bruce said, "if it wasn't for the wind blowing."

Nick was walking around with Jack Simmons at his side. They were looking at the ground, poking their toes into the soft dirt. I heard a beer can hit the asphalt.

I got Karen out and Bruce came around, repositioning his recorder on the seat I'd just left. I walked after some of them, slowing down as they fanned out over the wide, desolate intersection. The wind was coming across the top of the slopes—making sounds in the weeds. The air seemed to creak.

The sky was different—clouds were coming over, making a haze. It felt warm but the air had a chill in it somewhere. Nick was standing a dozen yards ahead. He walked a ways on top of the asphalt, then turned around, his hands outstretched.

"Here's right about where he hit," he announced. He looked up and down the road and walked around the area for moments, his head bent close to the pavement. "Here's the skids," he said. "Man, you can still see the skids. Can you believe it?"

Bruce was at his side, taking pictures now close to the road.

"You're exactly right," he said to Nick.

"They come all the way down here," Nick said, "then they stop—see, then jump, sort of, off at this angle—"

"And go over this way," Bruce said.

"Way over that way where the car was sitting after the wreck."

Jack was on the shoulder of the road—he looked small and was bending in a kind of curve with the wind blowing against his back. He wasn't moving, as though he wasn't going to set his foot on the asphalt.

Bruce wandered toward the shoulder, going farther west as Karen came close to me, digging at the ground with the toe of her shoe in much the same way as a couple of the others were doing. Sue was now deep in the ditch, digging and sifting the earth with a piece of wood.

Nick wanted to know where she'd found the stick. She said it was in the car.

"What's wrong?" Karen asked me. "Don't you want to look for something?"

"Are you kidding?" I said.

"Hey!" the albino cried. "I think this is a piece of the car—"

Sue was quickly upon it. Nick hurried back and looked at what they'd found. "No, it isn't," he said. "I can tell that metal a mile away. There might be pieces over there," he said, pointing off to the others. He then went on his own search, soon down on his hands and knees and digging into the loose earth. I stood there smoking a cigarette and after a few minutes Nick came up with a piece of red reflector—like glass.

"Part of a taillight," I said.

"It's not a piece of a Porsche," he said.

"What've you got?" Bruce asked.

"I don't know," Nick said.

"Looks like a bicycle reflector," I said, and thought, *You bunch of goddamn freaks*. I'd always thought of Nick as stupid—a blow-hard big-mouth fake. There he was—stupid, on the ground with some kid's busted piece of a handlebar.

I wanted to tell them they were all assholes. It was bubbling in my throat. Karen saw and took hold of my arm as if gaining balance. "You look sick," she said.

"There's been a thousand people tracking through here," Bruce said. "Last couple of times it's been the same—" He glanced at Jack who was walking back to the hearse. "That wrecking guy who has the Spyder. He's charging fifty cents to get a look at it."

"He's going cross-country in a big van," Nick said.

Sue said, "There's supposed to be a bloody handprint on the side of the car."

"That was grease," I said. "I heard it was grease. The car was pushed around when it was picked up. They're lying if they say it was blood."

Jack had climbed into the hearse. He called out, "Let's go! I'm going! It's too cold out here. Are you coming?"

He rolled up the window before anyone answered.

"Here's where Wutherich was," Nick said, "according to the medics." He walked around. "Here—No, wait, over here." He looked like Harpo Marx. "Here's where he was, lying on his back."

I looked down at the ground. I looked up at the sky. Karen's fingers were sinking into my arm. I was bending over—dizzy. I thought I might puke. I heard the hearse starting up. Jack was taking off.

Sue was running past us. She had pieces of tin in her hands to scoop the dirt. "If you take deep breaths you'll feel better," she said. "It always makes me carsick to ride so far."

I looked at her. I couldn't see her face. The sun was overhead. Her blonde hair was mussed and moving about her head like smoke. The face was blocked out by shadow.

It was like the sun was a huge vacuum sweeper and had just

sucked her up. Others were on their hands and knees in the dirt. Dust was blowing from their hands. I thought I'd pass out and I sat on the ground.

Karen squatted uncomfortably beside me. Her face was inches from mine. I wanted to kiss her. I said, "Did you love him?"

"You know I did," she said.

"I know you wanted to. I know it's the reason you're having the baby."

Tears were in her eyes. "I wanted this baby so he'd be with me. Now he's gone."

"He just came and went, didn't he?" I said, snapping my fingers. "That fast. Like that. Right here...."

"Yes," she said.

I looked down at the ground between my legs. "Maybe just seeing that car and hitting the brake—who knows..."

"I don't think he knew he was going to die," she said, trying not to let the others see the tears on her face.

"I think he knew," I said.

"No, he didn't," she said.

"Some part of him knew," I said. "It was that fast. Like a shot from a gun. He didn't even have time to know in his conscious mind—"

"Do you think he felt pain?" She was looking down and began digging her fingers into the earth.

"I don't know what he felt," I said. "It was too fast—"

"He always felt pain," she said. "Maybe that's all he felt—really—inside of himself. I feel like I want to open a floodgate in myself—I don't have enough tears. I don't have enough grief....We betrayed him."

"What's that mean?" I asked.

"Look at these people—sniveling around for our pieces of silver—a silver car. Here. What's this?" she said. She came up with something in her hand.

Jonathan Gilmore, Hollywood Hills Cafe 1996. Still riding with the shadow.

A piece of metal. It was silver—light, like a shred of a plane's fuselage. She brushed at it.

"It's a piece of the car," I said.

She stopped crying. She looked amazed. "A piece of the car!"

"Yeah," I said. "You've got a piece of the car...."